WORTHY
Exercise & Step book
{all in one}

DOUGLAS WEISS, PH.D.

Worthy: Exercise and Step book {all in one}
Copyright © 2016 by Douglas Weiss, Ph.D.

Requests for information:
Discovery Press
heart2heart@xc.org
719-278-3708

Interior and Cover designed by Janelle Evangelides
Edited by: Jim Kochenburger at Christianwriterhelp.com

Printed in the United States of America
ISBN # 978-1-881292-35-7

No portion of this material may be reproduced in any form or by any means without written permission of the author.

WEEK ONE   09

THE JOURNEY

(Refer to Disc One, Chapter One)

DAY ONE: HOW I GOT THERE	10
DAY TWO: IN THE BEGINNING	13
DAY THREE: THE OTHER SIDE	15
DAY FOUR: PLACES	17
DAY FIVE: DAILY TIME FOR RECOVERY	18

WEEK TWO   20

THE PURPOSE OF WORTHLESS

(Refer to Disc One, Chapter Two)

DAY ONE: WORTHLESS AS SAFETY	21
DAY TWO: CALL SOMEONE	23
DAY THREE: GOING TO WORTHY GROUPS	24
DAY FOUR: EVENING PRAYER	25
DAY FIVE: MAXIMIZED THINKING	28

WEEK THREE   29

WORTHLESS AS A FRIEND

(Refer to Disc One, Chapter Three)

DAY ONE: WORTHLESS AS A FRIEND	30
DAY TWO: STEP ONE	32
DAY THREE: WHAT WORTHLESS GAVE TO ME	34
DAY FOUR: EMPTY CHAIR	35
DAY FIVE: WHY?	37

WEEK FOUR   39

WORTHLESS AS AN ENEMY

(Refer to Disc One, Chapter Four)

DAY ONE: WORTHLESS AS AN ENEMY	40
DAY TWO: WORTHLESS KEEPS YOU STUCK	42

DAY THREE: WHO DISAGREES?	44
DAY FOUR: BOUNDARY	47
DAY FIVE: STEP TWO	51

WEEK FIVE — 53
WORTHLESS AS AN ADDICTION
(Refer to Disc One, Chapter Five)

DAY ONE: WORTHLESS AS AN ADDICTION	54
DAY TWO: LESS THAN	56
DAY THREE: EQUAL TO	58
DAY FOUR: THE OTHER PROBLEM	60
DAY FIVE: MENTOR	61

WEEK SIX — 62
WORTHLESSNESS AND GOD
(Refer to Disc One, Chapter Six)

DAY ONE: WORTHLESSNESS AND GOD	63
DAY TWO: IDENTIFYING AND COMMUNICATING FEELINGS	67
DAY THREE: STEP FOUR	71
DAY FOUR: STEP FIVE	74
DAY FIVE: MY FAMILY	78

WEEK SEVEN — 80
BECOMING WORTHY
(Refer to Disc Two, Chapter One)

DAY ONE: BECOMING WORTHY	81
DAY TWO: STEP SIX	82
DAY THREE: DATING	83
DAY FOUR: BODY	85
DAY FIVE: SEX EXCHANGE	86

WEEK EIGHT 88
SENSE OF WORTH
(Refer to Disc Two, Chapter Two)

- DAY ONE: SENSE OF WORTH — 89
- DAY TWO: STEP SEVEN — 90
- DAY THREE: ABUSE AND NEGLECT — 91
- DAY FOUR: WHAT YOU DID TO ME — 93
- DAY FIVE: MY PARENTING — 95

WEEK NINE 96
BREAKING THE AGREEMENT
(Refer to Disc Two, Chapter Three)

- DAY ONE: BREAKING THE AGREEMENT — 97
- DAY TWO: DAD CHAIR — 100
- DAY THREE: MY RELATIONSHIP WITH MOM — 100
- DAY FOUR: MOM CHAIR — 103
- DAY FIVE: STEP EIGHT — 104

WEEK TEN 105
STEPPING INTO WORTH
(Refer to Disc Two, Chapter Four)

- DAY ONE: STEPPING INTO WORTH — 106
- DAY TWO: SHAME — 107
- DAY THREE: I LEARNED — 108
- DAY FOUR: SECRETS — 109
- DAY FIVE: STEP NINE — 111

WEEK ELEVEN 113
DREAM
(Refer to Disc Two, Chapter Five)

AY ONE: DREAM	114
DAY TWO: FORGIVING YOURSELF	115
DAY THREE: WHO I OBEY	117
DAY FOUR: TEN THINGS	118
DAY FIVE: STEP TEN	120

WEEK TWELVE 121
LEGACY
(Refer to Disc Two, Chapter Six)

DAY ONE: WHAT IS NEW	122
DAY TWO: BEING CHOSEN	123
DAY THREE: HE ATTACKS	125
DAY FOUR: STEP ELEVEN	126
DAY FIVE: STEP TWELVE	127

STEP SECTION 129

STEP ONE	129
STEP TWO	136
STEP THREE	141
STEP FOUR	147
STEP FIVE	152
STEP SIX	156
STEP SEVEN	163
STEP EIGHT	168
STEP NINE	173
STEP TEN	179
STEP ELEVEN	182
STEP TWELVE	185
APPENDIX	189

Introduction

Welcome to the *Worthy Workbook*—and work is what it will be. You will be writing, thinking, and feeling; and you will be challenged. If the lies of worthlessness have sneaked into your soul and started to grow, then it means that worthlessness has roots somewhere in your life.

In the following pages, I will be asking you to do yourself a very large favor: *do the work!* It will not only change your life but it also has the potential to change the many lives you influence.

As you move into your worthy position in Christ, you will inspire others to be free and feel worthy as well. This battle is not only worth fighting for yourself and for those you love, it's also worth winning!

This workbook is laid out by sections, exercises, and Steps. The Steps section in the back is for those of you who believe your feelings of worthlessness are similar to an addiction. You can go through this workbook at your own pace or, if you are in a Worthy Group, go at the group's pace.

This workbook has been a labor of love. I have seen countless people move from worthlessness to worthy, and their lives have inspired me to write this. What you have here is a path that anyone can take. And that includes *you*. Follow this path, and you too will make the journey from worthless to worthy, just as others have.

We have created a Worthy Leaders Guide, for those walking through this journey together.

Download this free resource at: www.drdougweiss.com/worthy-leaders-guide

(•••) This symbol throughout the workbook is for suggested group discussion.

Douglas Weiss, Ph.D.

The Journey
(Refer to Disc One, Chapter One)

FILL OUT DURING DVD SESSION:

1. The voice of worthlessness is in your h_____.

2. Worthy is a j_____.

3. W_____ affects the way you think, feel, or behave.

4. Worthless is a l_____.

5. Worthless disagrees with the h_____ of God.

6. You are worthy because H_____ said so.

7. This process is w_____.

8. You are worthy r_____ of what has happened to you.

NOTES:
_____
_____
_____
_____
_____
_____
_____
_____

DAY ONE
HOW I GOT HERE

The voice of worthless can cripple you, even if you have a good community around you. Once worthless has come into your life, it can infiltrate every area. You will begin to question everything.

> **QUOTE**
>
> YOU ARE WORTHY
> YOU ARE A CHILD OF GOD
> YOU ARE WORTHY SPIRITUALLY
> YOU ARE WORTHY EMOTIONALLY
> YOU ARE WORTHY FINANCIALLY
> YOU ARE WORTHY SEXUALLY
> YOU ARE WORTHY AS A PARENT
> YOU ARE WORTHY AS A SPOUSE
> YOU ARE WORTHY AS A CHILD
> YOU ARE WORTHY, BECAUSE YOU ARE, BECAUSE HE SAYS SO.

You will need to recognize that the worthless voice has been speaking lies over you. Start to take a journey towards worthy and begin to believe and walk in the truth that you are worthy.

💬 What does your spirit say when you feel worthy?

_____
_____
_____
_____
_____
_____
_____
_____

You're worthy to:

_____
_____
_____
_____
_____
_____
_____
_____

💬 Write down your own story.

_____
_____
_____
_____
_____
_____
_____
_____
_____
_____
_____
_____
_____
_____

💬 What were the events that led you to generalize that you were worthless?

1. _____
2. _____
3. _____
4. _____
5. _____
6. _____
7. _____

MY STORY

MY STORY TOWARDS WORTHY, IS NOT WHAT YOU MIGHT THINK, I DIDN'T HAVE THE "PERFECT" PARENTS THAT TOLD ME I WAS LOVED EVERY DAY. I WAS CONCEIVED IN ADULTERY, NOT EXACTLY THE MOST "WORTHY" PLACE TO START. THIS CAUSED THE END OF MY MOTHERS FIRST MARRIAGE, THE GUY THAT GOT HER PREGNANT ABANDONED HER. I HAVE NEVER MET MY BIOLOGICAL FATHER. I WAS PUT IN FOSTER HOMES, ABANDONED BY MY MOM. I WAS SEXUALLY ABUSE AND ADDICTED TO DRUGS, ALCOHOL AND SEX. I WAS OUT OF CONTROL UNTIL CHRIST CAME INTO MY LIFE AND I BEGIN TO BREAK FREE FROM THE ADDICTIONS AND I'VE BEEN FREE NOW FOR OVER THIRTY YEARS.

Write about your family of origin experienced.

_____
_____
_____
_____
_____

Write about any abuse experience(s).

_____
_____
_____
_____
_____

Write about any sexual abuse experience(s).

_____
_____
_____
_____
_____

Write about any abortion experience(s).

_____
_____
_____
_____
_____

Write about your first sexual encounter.

_____
_____
_____
_____
_____

💬 Write about bad choices you've made.

_____
_____
_____
_____

Write about your sexual secrets.

_____
_____
_____
_____

💬 If you are married, write about your marriage and how its affected you in believing you are worthless.

_____
_____
_____
_____
_____
_____

DAY TWO
IN THE BEGINNING

I always wanted to start a book with the words, "In the beginning," so this is it! In the beginning God made all of us worthy. But sin stole that gift and continues to steal it from so many believers.

As we take the journey toward worthy together, I think we should start with defining it, but not the way a dictionary defines it; rather, I want you to define worthy how you have defined it in the past.

Write the first thing that comes to your mind, without thinking much about it, in the spaces provided.

In the past, I believed someone was worthy if:

1. _____
2. _____
3. _____
4. _____
5. _____

WHAT WOULD HAPPEN IF YOU BELIEVED YOU WERE WORTHY?

_____
_____
_____
_____

HOW WOULD YOU LIVE DIFFERENTLY IF YOU BELIEVED YOU WERE WORTHY?

_____
_____
_____
_____

NEXT

After completing the five items in the previous exercise, check the boxes below that indicate what you learned about your personal definition of worthy.

Was it any of the below? (Check)

☐ Attractiveness
☐ If I was told this by the opposite sex
☐ Body Image
☐ If I had sex with someone
☐ Finances
☐ My abilities
☐ Possessions
☐ If I was liked

3. Sometimes we must acknowledge the lies we believe before we can walk in the truth. What has been the message in your past that you have either been taught or believed about your worth? Write it here:

_____
_____
_____

MY CHOICE

Today you are a worthy man or woman of God. That's true, regardless of your beliefs or behavior. You have a choice to define what you want to believe worthy is.

In the space below write down how you would like to define worthy.

Worthy is:

1. _____
2. _____
3. _____
4. _____
5. _____

DAY THREE
THE OTHER SIDE

In the past, you would have had ideas about the opposite of worthy. You would have had some concepts about people, including yourself; you would have thought that some people are worth less than others.

Without much thought, write down some of your ideas of worthlessness as it pertains to others.

I believed someone was worthless if:

1. _____
2. _____
3. _____
4. _____
5. _____

MY PAST

Worthlessness is a nagging old voice the enemy of your soul has taunted you with for many years. However, this enemy uses "worthless" to interpret events from your life. What are some of the events that worthless has spoken to you?

> **ONCE WORTHLESS CAMPS INTO YOUR HEART IT BEGINS TO INFILTRATE DIFFERENT AREAS OF YOUR LIFE.**
>
> **YOU BEGIN TO QUESTION WHETHER YOU ARE WORTHY OF GOD'S LOVE.**
>
> **STOP BELIEVING THE LIE YOU ARE WORTHY!**

You feel worthless because:

1. _____
2. _____
3. _____
4. _____
5. _____
6. _____
7. _____
8. _____
9. _____
10. _____
11. _____
12. _____

What is the general message worthless speaks to your heart?

_____
_____
_____
_____
_____

DAY FOUR
PLACES

I live in Colorado. Here we do crazy things that don't make sense to outsiders. For example, we climb or scale mountains. I don't mean we hike along a path. I mean we use ropes and scale up massive rocks.

When you scale a mountain you learn one rule very quickly. You make sure that what you're about to put your weight on is secure. If it's secure, you can rest your full weight on it and move forward. If not, you could get scraped on the rocks, slide down, or even fall to your death.

Think of some people or things in your past on which you have placed your "weight," people or things in which you have placed your worth:

1. _____   4. _____
2. _____   5. _____
3. _____   6. _____

ROCK SOLID

> **MY STORY**
>
> MY ABANDONMENT, ABUSE, AND ADDICTION WERE TELLING ME I WAS WORTHLESS.
>
> HIS BLOOD WAS TELLING ME I WAS WORTHY.
>
> I WASN'T WORTHY BECAUSE OF WHAT I DID. I WAS WORTHY BECAUSE OF WHAT HE DID.

I remember being in my dorm room in Bible college, having gotten radically saved just a few weeks prior to admission. That "I'm not worthy" voice began to talk to me. The Lord spoke to me loud and clear and asked me one simple question that changed my life. "Who are you going to believe, them or me?"

He died, bled, and rose from the dead for me. He saved me to live with Him forever. Free from that day forward, I believed I was worthy of His blood because He said so.

This belief in His blood is rock solid in me. The blood doesn't change in value based on my past, present, or future circumstances. His blood is my value and my worth, and it is unshakeable and unmovable.

💬 What do you think about this idea? Do you believe you are worth the blood of Christ?

_____
_____
_____

Why or why not?

_____
_____

DAY FIVE
DAILY TIME FOR RECOVERY

Becoming a person who sees yourself as worthy isn't easy. That's because believing and receiving that you are innately worthy is hard work. More important, it is consistent work. Remember, it took consistent behaviors to spiral you into believing you were worthless in the past. It only makes sense that consistent work is going to be a big part of your beliefs for receiving that you are innately worthy.

In light of this, you are going to need time to practice many of the exercises in this workbook daily, which will grow you into an amazing, worthy person of God. These exercises are proven; they work successfully, but only if you take the time to do them. This is consistent with the fact that in most areas of life what you put into something is also what you get out of it. So, you may need to have a daily calendar and try to come up with at least fifteen to thirty minutes a day to work on your worth. This effort will make a big difference in the length of time it will take you to begin receiving that, believing that, and behaving like you are worthy.

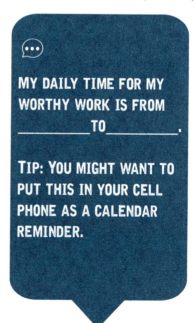

MY DAILY TIME FOR MY WORTHY WORK IS FROM _____ TO _____.

TIP: YOU MIGHT WANT TO PUT THIS IN YOUR CELL PHONE AS A CALENDAR REMINDER.

EARLY PRAYER

Take time out to pray first thing in the morning. If you need help, just use the guidelines of the Lord's Prayer (Matthew 6:9-13). During your prayer time, do not forget to ask Jesus to help you to receive and walk in your worthiness, and to stay accountable and honest today, so you can stay worthy. He is proud of you for starting to address this issue in your life. His death purchased your worth. Your prayer can help you realize how He sees you on a daily basis.

> "OUR FATHER IN HEAVEN, HALLOWED BE YOUR NAME, YOUR KINGDOM COME, YOUR WILL BE DONE, ON EARTH AS IT IS IN HEAVEN.
>
> GIVE US TODAY OUR DAILY BREAD. AND FORGIVE US OUR DEBTS, AS WE ALSO HAVE FORGIVEN OUR DEBTORS.
>
> AND LEAD US NOT INTO TEMPTATION, BUT DELIVER US FROM THE EVIL ONE."
>
> MATTHEW 6:9-13 (NIV)

Prayer is a way for you to behaviorally change yourself. For many who struggle with worthlessness, that accusing voice can start attacking you early in the day—not necessarily the first thing in the morning but maybe in the shower, on the way to work, or while driving. Prayer is preventative. It is a way of acknowledging you are worthy.

Those who struggle with worthlessness are in a fight every day, especially the first thirty to ninety days, which is the toughest period of renewing your mind. So make sure you connect with Jesus. Your prayer doesn't have to be long. Prayer may or may not make you feel better instantly, but it is one of the Five Commandments, which we will be discussing in a later exercise. If you begin to apply them to your life, you will begin to reap the benefits. As a Christian, prayer is one of the many tools you have to help you receive that you are worthy.

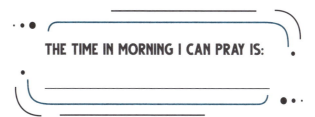

THE TIME IN MORNING I CAN PRAY IS:

WEEK TWO

The Purpose of Worthless
(Refer to Disc one, Chapter Two)

FILL OUT DURING DVD SESSION:

1. Worthless is w_____ for you in some way.

2. Your purpose for worthy might be the k_____ to your freedom.

3. I can't get rid of worthless until I am ready to exchange it for

   s_____ e_____.

4. Worthless s_____ you.

5. When you find out how worthless is serving you, then you can

   f_____ worthless.

6. Worthless could be assigned to keep you s_____.

7. When you have worthless as your core processing, your thinking has to be

   i_____ at times.

NOTES:

_____
_____
_____
_____
_____
_____
_____

DAY ONE
WORTHLESS AS SAFETY

A common way that worthless serves you is by protecting you. In order for you to feel safe, you have assigned worthless the task of keeping you safe. If this has happened, you will need to do some work to get through this. I encourage you to invite the Holy Spirit into this part of your heart.

How does worthless protect you? Give examples if this applies to you.

_____

_____

If safety applies to you, list some examples.

1. _____   4. _____
2. _____   5. _____
3. _____   6. _____

WORTHLESS AS A FUEL

Some people use worthless as a fuel to do better, such as get an education to get a better job. From the outside it looks good. It's okay to be high functioning, to strive for success, but it should not be at the expense of other things in your life. Shifting from worthless to worthy can be challenging in this situation, because worthless is what has fueled you to succeed and you will need to replace worthless with worthy.

(...) If worthless has fueled you to succeed, list several ways:

1. _____   4. _____
2. _____   5. _____
3. _____   6. _____

WORTHLESS CAN KEEP YOU FROM MAKING MISTAKES

Do you always apologize even for things you haven't done wrong or never apologize, because you simply cannot be wrong? This is a dangerous mindset to have. Worthless will give you the mindset that everything has to be perfect.

💬 If you have used worthless to keep you from making mistakes, list them below:

1. _____   4. _____

2. _____   5. _____

3. _____   6. _____

WORTHLESS CAN KEEP YOU FEELING UNWANTED

If worthless has you believing you are unwanted, you tend to reject everyone before they can reject you. If you have the fear of rejection or have the mindset of feeling unwanted, worthless can keep you believing you are unwanted so that you can be all alone and no one will question your judgement or see your flaws.

How does worthless keep you feeling unwanted?

1. _____   4. _____

2. _____   5. _____

3. _____   6. _____

💬 Check any of these traits of worthless that apply to you.

☐ Keeps you from being intimate.

☐ Keeps you from being intimate sexually.

☐ Keeps you depressed.

☐ Keeps you from trying.

☐ Keeps you from being responsible for your life.

☐ Keeps you in an addiction.

> **YOU DO NOT HAVE TO LIVE IN THE MINDSET THAT YOUR MISTAKES OR LACK OF MISTAKES DEFINE YOUR WORTH.**

DAY TWO
CALL SOMEONE

A phone call can be the very thing that may save you from dipping into worthless thoughts or behaviors today.

As a Christian, you know the body has many parts. You need another person with whom you can check in and be accountable. Remember, James 5:16 says: "Confess your faults...so you may be healed." The reverse is also true. Keep your faults (secret thoughts, behaviors) to yourself, and you will stay sick! When you believe or behave in a worthless manner, you keep yourself sick. You must push past your comfort zone to become and stay healthy. There are no Lone Rangers in the Christian walk, and there are definitely no lone rangers in becoming worthy if worthlessness has had a stronghold in your life. Remember, if you humble yourself, you can be free and experience the true feelings of being worthy.

A lifestyle of beliefs or feelings is a much greater goal than living in the past, like you have. There are several ways to address this commandment about making phone calls. One way is to wait until you get into crisis mode, and then call someone to help you. This method does not work, because if you don't have a relationship with anyone, then you could put up a barrier that would isolate you and make it difficult to call someone when needed. Making a phone call and saying, "I am being attacked by worthless," is a big enough task all by itself to accomplish.

When you are not alone, you are accountable. The way to begin making phone calls is to make one in the morning to a person to whom you can be accountable. Tell them that if you have feelings of worthlessness today, then you will call someone. If you are "checked in," then eventually the phone calls are going to turn into conversations, which will develop healthy relationships.

> **WHEN YOU HAVE WORTHLESS AS A CORE BELIEF, YOUR REASONING CAN'T ALWAYS BE RATIONAL.**

We all need relationships. Part of the battle is making phone calls, feeling connected and getting acceptance right at the beginning of the day. If you can make a phone call early in the morning you are going to find strength in your day. Like prayer, the phone is a tool you can use to help yourself get stronger, especially within the first thirty to ninety days when you are going to need other people to help you more than ever before. The people you call will benefit just as much, if not more, than you will. Make a phone call every day. You do not need to philosophically agree with this concept or have a good feeling about it to decide if you are going to do it. This phone call behavior is so that you can get and stay worthy for the rest of your life.

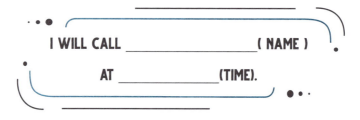

I WILL CALL _____ (NAME)
AT _____ (TIME).

DAY THREE
GOING TO WORTHY GROUPS

In Alcoholics Anonymous there is an old expression that says, "There are three times when you should go to a meeting: when you don't feel like going to a meeting, when you do feel like going to a meeting, and at eight o'clock." It is not a matter of how you feel about it. It is how you behave about it. In the midst of a tough situation, when you are far removed from a worthy group or accountability partner, it can be more difficult. If this happens to you, you may want to consider talking with a support person more frequently as an option. Or you can start a Worthy Group in your church.

> "THEREFORE CONFESS YOUR SINS TO EACH OTHER AND PRAY FOR EACH OTHER SO THAT YOU MAY BE HEALED.
>
> THE PRAYER OF A RIGHTEOUS PERSON IS POWERFUL AND EFFECTIVE."
>
> JAMES 5:16 (NIV)

If you are interested in starting a Worthy Group in your church, please contact us so we can refer people to your group. If it isn't possible to start a Worthy Group, and there are none available in your area, then a Bible study, Celebrate Recovery, or Recovery For Everyone group can be helpful when you need just to be honest about your issues surrounding worthy. It is our belief that God wants to use His church to heal those who struggle with worthlessness in the church, as well as in the community. If the church will open its healing doors, I believe we will see no less than a revival!

These meetings are basically to support you and, at some point, to help you give back to others what you have learned through your own particular journey of believing and becoming worthy. Being around other people on the same journey is going to help you. How? First, it is going to give you hope as you see others grow and change as they accept the worth Christ has given to them. Second, if they can do it, you may believe you can too. You can learn things from them, which they have learned through negative or positive experiences. I want to encourage you to attend as many groups as possible.

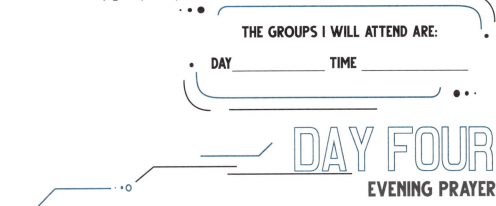

THE GROUPS I WILL ATTEND ARE:

DAY_____ TIME _____

DAY FOUR
EVENING PRAYER

Praying again in the evening may sound redundant. Prayer is something that is best to do twice, at a minimum, every day. At the end of the day, if you were able to shake the claws of worthlessness and embrace the worthiness that God has given to you in Christ, then thank God. Every day of worthy is a miracle to personally thank Jesus for.

If there are any other issues from your day you want to talk with God about, you can bring them up at this time as well. It is important to begin and end your day in a spiritual place. The healing from worthlessness is spiritual in nature. Since you were born spirit, soul, and body, it is important to engage your spirit on this journey of worthy. Some who struggle with worthlessness don't nurture their spirit even though they are Christians. Make this a time to be thankful that you had a day of believing and behaving in a worthy manner.

THE FIVE COMMANDMENTS - A NINETY-DAY CHECKLIST

Healing from worthless behavior has some basic principles that, when applied, help you sustain being and staying worthy. Early healing is not simply about understanding the facts; nor is early healing simply talking about the problem. Healing goes much deeper than simply talking about what was done in the past. Many Christians may talk about getting better. The Prodigal Son, who probably had some worthy issues, did not get better or become restored when he realized he was in a bad condition. He had to consistently walk back in order to receive the blessings of his healing, which took weeks, if not months. It was then that the welcome-home party started, not before.

The Five Commandments are simple and can be posted on your wall or mirror at home. Write the commandments down and check off if you have done them each day for the first ninety days. The behavioral checklist assures that you are taking steps toward becoming worthy and behaving as if you are worthy, instead of just coming to an understanding about the problem. "Understanding" is not the only answer for you while you're moving toward believing and behaving like you are worthy. It is for this reason the Five Commandments, when put in place, can provide an action plan.

These Five Commandments are simple:

THE FIVE COMMANDMENTS

Commandment #1 - Pray in the morning
Commandment #2 - Read helpful material daily
Commandment #3 - Attend meetings
Commandment #4 - Call someone
Commandment #5 - Pray again and thank God

This checklist will help you monitor your behavior. When it comes to believing and behaving like you are worthy, remember, believe your behaviors only. Don't talk yourself into believing that you feel free—you are free. Behave free, and you will be.

Date	Pray	Read	Meet	Call	Pray	Date	Pray	Read	Meet	Call	Pray
1.						46.					
2.						47.					
3.						48.					
4.						49.					
5.						50.					
6.						51.					
7.						52.					
8.						53.					
9.						54.					
10.						55.					
11.						56.					
12.						57.					
13.						58.					
14.						59.					
15.						60.					
16.						61.					
17.						62.					
18.						63.					
19.						64.					
20.						65.					
21.						66.					
22.						67.					
23.						68.					
24.						69.					
25.						70.					
26.						71.					
27.						72.					
28.						73.					
29.						74.					
30.						75.					
31.						76.					
32.						77.					
33.						78.					
34.						79.					
35.						80.					
36.						81.					
37.						82.					
38.						83.					
39.						84.					
40.						85.					
41.						86.					
42.						87.					
43.						88.					
44.						89.					
45.						90.					

DAY FIVE
MAXIMIXED THINKING

The maximized thinking technique is easy to understand. Simply ask yourself daily, especially during the first sixty to ninety days on your worthy journey, "Is this the most I can put into my journey today?" If the answer is more "yes" than "no" you will find yourself progressing through your journey to worthy quite well. Maximized thinking plays a big part in the early stages of the journey toward worthy.

Those who consistently maintain the Five Commandments as much as possible will make tremendous gains with maximized thinking. I have watched as those who struggle with worthlessness have chosen maximized thinking in their journey and experienced a much healthier lifestyle.

Other options are shades of minimized thinking. It may be characterized by those who ask themselves "How little can I do?" to show others they are trying to get better. This type of minimized thinking is done mostly on a less-than-conscious level and can be measured by a lack of doing the work of healing.

One way I determine the level of seriousness in the early part of the journey is by behaviors. Intention, no matter how good, misleads you to think you are making progress when you actually are not. The Five Commandments is a good way to determine if you are applying maximized thinking or some other approach to what may be the hardest task of your life—breaking the shackles of worthlessness. If you are still reading up to this point, that is a good sign, but keep going! Your life can be ten to one hundred times better than any day of living actively in a worthless lifestyle.

Remember, you have not resisted sin unto death, as Christ has for us. Think, "What is the best I can do to become and stay free for Him, since He has given His best for me?"

> **QUOTE**
>
> **FREEDOM FROM WORTHLESSNESS ISN'T SOMETHING YOU DO BY YOURSELF. IT IS SOMETHING YOU DO WITH THE HELP OF GOD AND OTHERS.**

Worthless as a Friend
(Refer to Disc One, Chapter Three)

FILL OUT DURING DVD SESSION:

1. You have spent t_____ of hours with worthless.

2. You are f_____.

3. You can d_____ on worthless.

4. This friend has been with you a l_____ l_____ time.

5. Worthless would not be in your life if you were not in a_____. Amos 3:3

6. Maybe you needed worthless to s_____ but you have to get rid of worthless to l_____.

7. If you don't get rid of w_____ it can become part of your family.

NOTES:
_____
_____
_____
_____
_____
_____

DAY ONE
WORTHLESS AS A FRIEND

The voice of worthless has been with you in elementary school, junior high, high-school and into your adulthood, constantly telling you why you aren't worthy. Looking at worthless as a friend, I want you to write a thank you letter. Thank worthless for how it has been a friend to you in the past.

> **TRUST ME WHEN I SAY, "YOU ARE WORTHY." SO MAXIMIZE THE EARLY PART OF YOUR JOURNEY AND YOU WILL HAVE THE REST OF YOUR LIFE TO THANK YOURSELF FOR THE TIME YOU INVESTED.**

THANK YOU WORTHLESS,

_____
_____
_____
_____
_____
_____
_____
_____
_____
_____
_____
_____
_____
_____
_____
_____
_____
_____
_____
_____

As we begin to move away from worthless as a friend, it is important that you take a moment and put a crack in the relationship you have had with worthless. Because worthless has been a friend for so long in your life, you need to let it know that you no longer need or want to hear these voices in your head. You will now need to get rid of worthless so you can LIVE! If you do not say goodbye it will come into your family and your kids will begin to pick up these lies.

💬 GOODBYE WORTHLESS,

_____
_____
_____
_____
_____
_____
_____
_____
_____
_____
_____
_____
_____
_____
_____
_____
_____
_____
_____

> **QUOTE**
>
> **DECIDE TODAY TO SAY GOODBYE TO WORTHLESS AND PASS ON A LIFESTYLE WHERE YOUR KIDS AND GRANDKIDS KNOW IN THEIR HEART AND SOULS THAT THEY ARE WORTHY.**

DAY TWO
STEP ONE

"WE ADMITTED WE WERE POWERLESS OVER WORTHLESSNESS—THAT OUR LIVES HAD BECOME UNMANAGEABLE."

This is the most important step of all. In Step One, you place your feet on the path toward getting and staying free from worthlessness. "We" means you will have others involved with you in your journey. Healing from worthlessness is a team participation sport. "We admitted" is not a completion of Step One. Some people attend meetings and never complete Step One. Some simply admit they have "an issue" much like an alcoholic has when he or she is drinking beer.

> **IF YOU BELIEVE YOU HAVE BEEN ADDICTED TO WORTHLESSNESS THEN WE ENCOURAGE YOU TO DO THE STEPS WORKBOOK PORTION IN THE BACK OF THIS WORKBOOK. IF YOU DON'T THINK YOU ARE ADDICTED TO WORTHLESS, YOU CAN SKIP THE STEPS WORKBOOK PORTION OF THIS BOOK.**

Step One has us admit we are "powerless." Powerlessness is different from being in agreement with worthlessness. Being addicted to cocaine could mean that when you saw cocaine, "you couldn't help yourself," and you used the cocaine. Powerlessness would be if you saw cocaine, you would run out, call someone, and try any helpful behaviors to avoid what once controlled your life. If you're powerless over worthlessness when you feel or think worthlessly, then you get others to help you immediately. You regret the old familiar road of how worthless you feel and you instead get others to help you make a U-turn down Worthy Blvd.

Many lives are tainted with the unmanageability that worthlessness brings. In your journey, sanity and order will replace the "crazies" and chaos that worthlessness has brought into your life.

CHECK OFF THE BEHAVIORS YOU CURRENTLY HAVE THAT SUPPORT YOUR STEP ONE.

Behavior	Yes	No
1. Prayer	___	___
2. Reading	___	___
3. Phone calls	___	___
4. Meetings	___	___
5. Staying accountable with your thoughts and behaviors	___	___
6. Creativity in your journey to worthy	___	___

The day I completed my Second Step was _____

THE BRAIN PROBLEM

Any time you use your brain by turning it in a certain direction, you move toward creating a pattern. Over time if you are consistent with this behavior you create a habit. Many people who struggle with worthlessness have created a thought habit about themselves, such as "I can't," "I'm not good enough," "Nobody will love me," "I'm stupid," "I always lose," and so on.

These thoughts grieve the Holy Spirit for sure. He knows what it is like to create and sustain you and the unlimited gifts you have. So what should you do when you get a worthless thought?

One idea is to place a rubber band around your wrist for thirty days. Every time you think or speak a worthless statement, snap the rubber band. If you quote a positive scripture or thought after snapping the rubber band, that can be helpful as well. At first you will be snapping it quite a bit, but soon your brain will say, "Stop it!" and won't allow the negative patterns.

If after snapping a few times a thought persists, call someone. Tell them the lie you're thinking about and let them pray for you.

THE DAY I PLACED A RUBBER BAND ON MY WRIST WAS _____.

DAY THREE
WHAT WORTHLESS GAVE TO ME

Think about the relationship you have had with worthless and the voice it has been in your life. This relationship may have been decades in the making. You ran to worthless throughout your life and found worthless was always there for you. Worthless would give you the answer to try harder or the excuse not to try at all. Worthless has been your long-term friend and a well-established relationship for you.

I know it may be challenging to believe that worthless has been giving you something. However, you have kept this relationship going for decades so there has to be something that worthless is providing for you. Maybe it's been keeping you from things. Maybe you've been blaming it for issues in your life. Maybe it's helped you to not confront people or to accept less in areas of your life. Maybe it's kept you unemployed or prevented you from contributing to society. Maybe it's given you excuses for not engaging in life fully with your gifts or abilities. Maybe it's kept you afraid and helped you receive pity, help, or support from others.

It will take honesty and courage to make your list below about what worthless in the past has given you. This list can be helpful in your journey to worthy. To know what worthless was doing for you can help you get these needs or desires met in a worthy manner.

WHAT WORTHLESS TOOK FROM ME

For every relationship, you can create a list of losses and gains from it. In the relationship with worthless, what worthless has given to you over the decades is often smaller than what worthless has actually taken from you.

Worthless can take things from you that you don't see. They are things that worthless kept from happening. For instance, it kept you from starting a business, getting an education, waiting for sex. It kept you from saying no to abortions that would not have happened. It kept you from relationships you could have had, from a certain career, from a different relationship with your family or children than you have.

DAY FOUR
EMPTY CHAIR

The "empty chair" exercise has helped many clients in therapy not only to experience but also to further the work they have completed in the previous exercises. The deeper you go to confront your thoughts and feelings of worthlessness, the better sense of resolve you will experience, which may be the one tool that will help you remain in a worthy lifestyle.

In this exercise, you will sit in a chair. Place another empty chair directly in front of you, facing you. While sitting in the chair, be sure you have your thank you and goodbye letters you wrote to worthlessness with you. Read your letters out loud, as if worthlessness was a real person sitting in the chair in front of you. No one else needs to be there unless you want support from someone. For most of your life, worthlessness was a real person. Men's and women's experiences with this exercise have varied.

EXAMPLE:

In the space below, you can list your thoughts and feelings after completing this exercise.

MY THOUGHTS WERE:

_____
_____
_____
_____
_____
_____
_____
_____
_____
_____
_____
_____
_____
_____
_____
_____
_____
_____

MY FEELINGS WERE:

_____
_____
_____
_____
_____
_____
_____
_____
_____
_____
_____
_____
_____
_____
_____
_____
_____
_____

☐ **WHO AGREES?**

In your life you will have a variety of friends. Let's say you have a same-gender friend named Bob or Sue. People in your life, whether family or other friends, all are going to have their opinion about your friend Bob or Sue.

Some will like Bob or Sue, some won't like Bob or Sue—and for a variety of reasons. Your friend worthless has been there for decades. In this exercise I want you to name the people who like your friend worthless. Maybe worthless helps them take advantage of you or discount your worth or treat you less than respectfully. Think through your list—it might include friends, your spouse, an ex-spouse, neighbors, your family of origin, siblings, your children, or your employer.

THOSE WHO AGREE WITH WORTHLESS

1. _____
2. _____
3. _____
4. _____
5. _____
6. _____
7. _____
8. _____
9. _____
10. _____

DAY FIVE
WHY?

In the last exercise you made a list of people who like your friend worthless. They all have different reasons why they like worthless. In the spaces below write out your best guess as to why they like your friend worthless. Please write as much as you need to. Use a separate sheet of paper if necessary.

NAME: **REASON:**

1. _____ _____
2. _____ _____
3. _____ _____
4. _____ _____
5. _____ _____
6. _____ _____
7. _____ _____
8. _____ _____
9. _____ _____
10. _____ _____

I SHARED THIS WITH _____.

DRINKING BUDDIES

Addicts of every kind have what we call "drinking buddies." These buddies feed, reinforce, support, tolerate and never mention the addiction.

People who struggle with worthlessness also have drinking buddies—which you just listed in the last two exercises. In recovery, the addict has to change play places, play things, playmates. They have to drastically change or get out of these relationships all together to be able to heal from the addiction.

Write down the names of your worthless drinking buddies, if you need to end these relationships, and how you need to create boundaries or change the relationship.

NAME: **ACTION PLAN:**

1. _____ _____
2. _____ _____
3. _____ _____
4. _____ _____
5. _____ _____
6. _____ _____
7. _____ _____
8. _____ _____
9. _____ _____
10. _____ _____

I SHARED THIS WITH

_____.

WEEK FOUR

Worthless As An Enemy
(Refer to Disc One, Chapter Four)

FILL OUT DURING DVD SESSION:

1. Worthless is not from G_____.

2. We have to be in a_____ for things to have an impact on our lives.

3. What you L_____ is what you p_____.

4. If you protect worthless, you l_____ worthless.

5. Worthless is an enemy keeping you from who you are in C_____.

6. Worthless can affect your i_____ with the Father.

7. Worthless can keep you in your c_____ z_____.

NOTES:

_____
_____
_____
_____
_____
_____
_____
_____

DAY ONE
WORTHLESS AS AN ENEMY

I hate what worthless does to people. It cripples their mind, darkens their eyes, limits their strengths and keeps them stuck. Worthless is your enemy, it is not from God.

What you love, is what you protect. My hope is that through these exercises you will begin to take a stand against worthless and move into a position to stand against it, telling it has no authority in your life, and that you were created with a purpose.

ANGER LETTER TO WORTHLESS

This exercise takes you a step further into healing from the lies worthless has spoken over you. This anger letter is for your healing. In this exercise, imagine having worthless in a room, strapped to a chair. Imagine it can't say anything to you, and you can say anything and everything you want to it. To begin, write down all the feelings of anger, rage, hurt, and everything you wish you could tell worthless. Make this letter as long as you need it to be, using any language you feel you need to communicate the anger you have. To heal, you must get rid of the anger inside of you. You are worth the time and energy you will need to heal this anger.

(...) On separate paper, write your letter. Sharing this letter with your recovery friend or group member(s) will be helpful as well.

> **QUOTE**
>
> **YOUR DREAMS MATTER.**
> **YOUR STORY IS IMPORTANT.**
> **YOU ARE MORE THAN ENOUGH.**

ANGER WORK

You are probably familiar with the biblical story of Jesus engaging His anger when emptying the temple of those who were defiling it. Worthless has defiled your temple. Do not do this exercise without first writing the anger letter in the previous exercise. It will not be nearly as effective.

You will need a bat or solid racket of some kind and a mattress or a pillow for a target for this exercise. It will take about 1 and 1/2 hours of total alone time, so don't forget to turn off the phones and ensure that you will have complete privacy for the duration of this exercise.

It's very important that you follow these steps in order.

WARM UP, PART 1 - For the first round, warm up by taking the bat/racket and hitting the target with one small hit, then a medium hit, followed by a large hit and finally a very large hit. Round two is done the same, with two small hits, two medium hits, two large hits, and two very large hits. The third and final round consists of three hits each - small, medium, large, and extra-large.

WARM UP, PART 2 - Use your voice along with these hits. Use the word "no" in a quiet voice, a medium voice, a loud voice, and an extra loud voice while hitting the mattress or pillow with corresponding hits. Do all three rounds as in Part 1, but use your voice with the hits.

Following the warm up exercises, take your anger letter and read it aloud, as if your husband is in the room with you but unable to speak or react . Next, take your bat/racket and hit the target, saying the things you said in the letter and anything else that comes to mind. You may cry during the exercise, but this isn't the goal; stay angry during this time and you may get the relief you need as you verbally and physically express your anger.

This exercise usually only needs to be done one time. If you feel you didn't get what you needed or didn't let go of control enough, you can try again. If you feel you need help with this exercise, you can set up a telephone appointment. Instructions are in the back of this workbook for this service.

ANGER WORK STEPS

1. Get equipment and ensure privacy for yourself for the entire time
2. Warm up Part 1

	1st Round	2nd Round	3rd Round
Small hit	1 hit	2 hits	3 hits
Medium hit	1 hit	2 hits	3 hits
Large hit	1 hit	2 hits	3 hits
Extra large hit	1 hit	2 hits	3 hits

3. Warm Up Part 2 - add your voice to the above (small hit, small voice; medium hit/medium voice, etc.)
4. Read letter
5. Hit the bed/target - Say what you need to say, as loud and as long as you need to hit it/say it

Warning: If you have any medical conditions, consult your doctor before doing this exercise

DATE I COMPLETED THE ANGER LETTER AND ANGER WORK_____.

> **WORTHLESS IS SOMETHING WE NEED TO STAND AGAINST, GET ANGRY WITH AND AIM OUR SWORDS AT, INSTEAD OF KEEPING IT INSIDE AND PROTECTING IT.**

DAY TWO
WORTHLESS KEEPS YOU STUCK

Worthless is an enemy and is keeping you from who you are in Christ. Worthless robs you of becoming who you really are. It robs you of intimacy with your Heavenly Father. How can you be intimate with the Father, who says He loves you by sending his son to die for you and tells you that you are worthy of his blood and at the very same time, believe you are worthless? Your worth is based on something that cannot be moved. Your worth is based on His blood. His blood does not move, it does not change, it will always say, *"I love you, you are worthy of my death."*

💬 What are some of the things worthless has robbed from you?

1._____ 4._____
2._____ 5._____
3._____ 6._____

Have you let worthless affect intimacy with your Heavenly Father? If so, list how.

1._____ 4._____
2._____ 5._____
3._____ 6._____

Worthless will keep you from taking risks. You only grow when you take risks. Life begins when you get out of your comfort zone. If you are following Jesus, there is no such thing as a comfort zone, because He will continue to call you into something greater and bigger than you could have imagined.

💬 What risks have you not taken due to worthless?

1._____ 4._____
2._____ 5._____
3._____ 6._____

Worthless can keep you chained from moving. *"I can't move because I am worthless."* I want you to hear my heart. If you are hearing "I CAN'T" then worthless is still your friend. YOU CAN do all things through Christ. Your mind has to be changed and transformed to what He says about you!

In what way has worthless kept you chained from moving forward?

1._____
2._____
3._____
4._____

> **"I CAN DO ALL THINGS THROUGH CHRIST WHO STRENGTHENS ME."**
>
> **PHILLIPPIANS 4:13 (NIV)**

One of the things we want to move toward is thanking the Father for making us worthy and actually believing it! Last week you wrote a goodbye letter to worthless and one of the things you may have to do is pull it out weekly and read it and claim authority over worthless. When worthless becomes your enemy and you hear it pop-up in your heart, fight back.

My encouragement to you is that you begin to see worthless as an enemy. It might have been a friend in the past, but it is an enemy because it is preventing you from living the abundant life God has called you to achieve. Attack it like it is an enemy. Go through this workbook and be aggressive with every exercise because you are worthy and you deserve to be free!

DAY THREE
WHO DISAGREES?

You might like, love, cherish, and protect your friend worthless, but there may be people in your life who see how damaging this relationship really is to you.

THOSE WHO DISAGREE WITH WORTHLESS

1. _____
2. _____
3. _____
4. _____
5. _____
6. _____
7. _____
8. _____
9. _____
10. _____

I'm sure you know what it's like when a teenager starts hanging around the wrong type of friend and it changes him or her. Similarly there are probably people in your life who really *don't* like the worthless you're listening to and hanging around with.

Write their names, whether they are family members, a spouse, coworkers, friends, children, siblings, or neighbors.

 **WHY THEY DISAGREE**

You listed people who rightfully disagree with your relationship with worthlessness. In the spaces below, write out their names again, as well as their words or behaviors that gave you the message that they *don't* like your friend worthlessness.

NAME: **WORDS/BEHAVIORS:**

1. _____   _____
2. _____   _____
3. _____   _____
4. _____   _____
5. _____   _____
6. _____   _____
7. _____   _____
8. _____   _____
9. _____   _____
10. _____   _____

FRIENDS...

Now that you have made a list of probably your better friends, who are usually healthy people for you to be around, who don't like worthlessness. They themselves believe they have value and that others have value too. They would not agree with your self-deprecating humor, lack of acknowledgment of your value or your gifts, and your lack of boundaries with people close to you.

In the journey toward believing or behaving that you are innately worthy, there are spiritually and emotionally healthy people you want to have time with. Get their support and opinions. You will have to disagree with your old friend worthlessness, but that will be good for you.

In the space below, write their names and how you can increase your time with them and their influence in your life.

NAME: **ACTION PLAN:**

1. _____   _____
2. _____   _____
3. _____   _____
4. _____   _____
5. _____   _____
6. _____   _____
7. _____   _____
8. _____   _____
9. _____   _____
10. _____   _____

TRAINING THEM

As you grow on your journey toward worthy, there are beliefs and behaviors that you will have to pause and do something about. You are going to have to look at and accept the fact that you are 100 percent responsible for training others to treat you and talk to you in a worthy manner.

I know they are responsible for their behavior, but allowing it or even rewarding it by capitulating, being silent, not calling the police, not having boundaries, or accepting the way they talk to you in a less-than-respectful tone is 100 percent your responsibility. Allowing their behavior does not help them or you experience being worthy.

Go back to your list of people who like your friend worthless. Put their names below and write out an idea or two about how you need to start becoming different in that relationship so that you will be treated in a worthy manner.

NAME: **MY BEING DIFFERENT:**

1. _____   _____
2. _____   _____
3. _____   _____
4. _____   _____
5. _____   _____
6. _____   _____
7. _____   _____
8. _____   _____
9. _____   _____
10. _____   _____

DAY FOUR
BOUNDARY

A boundary says two things. First, a boundary says, "I have value." Second, a boundary says, "I can enforce consequences if this boundary is broken."

Some countries have solid boundaries, strong boundaries. Some countries' boundaries are weak. People are the same way.

As you move into more worthy beliefs and behaviors, you will need to not only understand but also maintain boundaries, *especially with those who you have trained to treat you poorly.*

> **A BOUNDARY IS SIMPLY PUTTING A LINE IN THE SAND AND VERBALLY DECLARING, "IF THIS BEHAVIOR OCCURS, THEN X WILL BE THE CONSEQUENCE."**

Once you establish a boundary with a person, you will most likely have to reinforce it several times until the other person accepts you have changed and that you're going to be consistent about maintaining your boundary.

In the space below write a few people's names and the boundaries that you need to implement for them. Here's an example for the friend who hangs up the phone on you.

NAME: Sue

MY BOUNDARY: If you hang up the phone on me I won't call you back or talk to you until you apologize for being disrespectful.

1. _____
2. _____
3. _____
4. _____
5. _____
6. _____
7. _____
8. _____
9. _____
10. _____

I SHARED THIS WITH _____ .

CONSEQUENCES

In the last exercise I alluded to the concept of consequences. But I want to elaborate. When you set a boundary you want to do this preferably *before* someone repeats a behavior.

When you set a boundary, be calm and just simply let them know if they do X behavior you will do or not do Y. When you set a consequence, you have to make it so *you* are doing or not doing something. The boundary requires no cooperation from them to keep your boundary.

A consequence is not a punishment. For example, if you say: "If you yell at me, then you have to do ten pushups." That's not realistic. You can't make someone do ten pushups. A consequence would be, "If you yell at me, then I am going to sleep in a different room tonight."

In the space below, write out a few ideas of boundaries and consequences. Then run this by someone else to see if you're getting the idea.

IDEAS FOR BOUNDARIES AND CONSEQUENCES:

1. _____
2. _____
3. _____
4. _____
5. _____
6. _____

I SHARED THIS WITH

_____ .

ONE AT A TIME

When someone starts feeling and believing worthy, he or she can get new energy for life and relationships. This zest for life and relationships is great and a sign that you are making progress in believing and behaving like a worthy person.

However, when it comes to boundaries, I strongly suggest you do only one boundary at a time. Don't give your spouse or child five new boundaries.

Let me give you an illustration from history. Adolf Hitler developed a war technique called *Blitzkrieg*. He would aim all his military forces, planes, tanks, and soldiers to one front of the war. He was invincible until he veered from his strategy and started to fight on two fronts. It was then that he lost the war.

So when you go to make a change in a relationship, go slow on one front at a time. Start at thirty to ninety days. Stay consistent with the consequence. When their behavior changes then, move to the next boundary.

NAME: **BOUNDARY:**

1. _____   _____
2. _____   _____
3. _____   _____
4. _____   _____
5. _____   _____
6. _____   _____
7. _____   _____
8. _____   _____
9. _____   _____
10. _____   _____

DAY FIVE
STEP TWO

"CAME TO BELIEVE A POWER GREATER THAN OURSELVES COULD RESTORE US TO SANITY."

Coming to believe in one power that is able to heal you is a process. As Christians, we know this power is Jesus Christ. So did the writer of the Twelve Steps. The first writing of the Twelve Steps used the word "God" in place of "power greater than ourselves." In the 1930s, they didn't think our culture would broaden this "power" to anything else. In current traditional Twelve Step groups (not recovery groups), they take this step too loosely; but in Step Three, they continue with the word "God." Remember, believing is behaving.

In Step Two, you are coming to believe God can and will heal you from worthlessness. It is His will that you put your faith in His voice, which says you are worthy, rather than the voice of worthlessness you have agreed with in the past.

CHECK OFF THE BEHAVIORS YOU CURRENTLY HAVE THAT SUPPORT YOUR STEP TWO.

Behavior	Yes	No
1. Honesty about your spiritual place	___	___
2. Prayer	___	___
3. Meditation	___	___
4. Bible reading	___	___
5. Dialoguing with others who you feel have a good relationship with Jesus	___	___

The day I completed my Second Step was _____

MY CONSEQUENCES

This is going to seem a little odd, but it is really important to have a consequence in place when you start addressing boundaries. Often, if you struggle with worthlessness, you will change your mind or simply not follow through. (This is what others will expect because of how you trained them.)

So you must have a consequence for yourself if you don't follow through. Be accountable to someone if you don't follow through with that consequence.

FOR EXAMPLE:
Boundary: If you yell at me...
Consequence: I will sleep in another room.
My Consequence: If I don't sleep in another room, I will clean all the toilets the next day.

You might feel like you don't need a consequence for yourself or accountability for your lack of follow-through, but in my experience your chances of relapsing into worthless behavior and having unhealthy people around you is much higher if you don't have a consequence.

What will be your consequence if you do not follow through with your boundary?

> **YOU HAVE TO BE WILLING AND ABLE TO FOLLOW THROUGH WITH A CONSEQUENCE THAT YOU CAN ENFORCE—WITHOUT THE OTHER PERSON'S ASSISTANCE.**

NAME	BOUNDARY	MY CONSEQUENCE
1. _____	_____	_____
2. _____	_____	_____
3. _____	_____	_____
4. _____	_____	_____
5. _____	_____	_____
6. _____	_____	_____
7. _____	_____	_____
8. _____	_____	_____
9. _____	_____	_____
10. _____	_____	_____

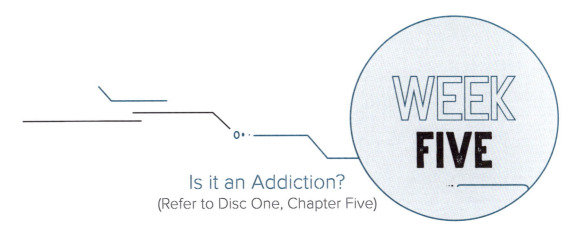

Is it an Addiction?
(Refer to Disc One, Chapter Five)

FILL OUT DURING DVD SESSION:

1. You can be a _____ to worthless.
2. E_____ to stop?
3. Fail after p_____?
4. Have you continued using w_____ ?
5. Have you had c_____?
6. Keep u_____ after the consequences?
7. Kept you from other a _____?
8. A_____ more and more time?
9. U_____ worthless more and more?

NOTES:
_____
_____
_____
_____
_____
_____
_____
_____
_____
_____

DAY ONE
WORTHLESS AS AN ADDICTION

Worthless like many other addictions is a process addiction. In over thirty years of counseling individuals from many different backgrounds, I have seen worthless as a very strong addiction and it may be the reason you are struggling to overcome worthlessness. You will need to look at the criteria to determine if worthless is an addiction for you.

Did you make efforts to stop?   ___Yes ___No
EXAMPLES:
_____
_____
_____
_____

Did you make promises to stop? ___Yes ___No
EXAMPLES:
_____
_____
_____
_____

Did you fail after promising? ___Yes ___No
EXAMPLES:
_____
_____
_____
_____

> **YOUR WORTH IS NOT DEFINED BY AN ADDICTION.**
> **IT'S NOT DEFINED BY YOUR PARENTS.**
> **IT'S NOT DEFINED BY THE ABUSE.**
> **IT'S NOT DEFINED BY DEPRESSION.**
> **IT'S NOT DEFINED BY BROKEN RELATIONSHIPS.**
>
> **YOU ARE WORTHY!**

Have you continued using worthless? ___Yes ___No

EXAMPLES:

_____
_____
_____
_____

Have you had consequences? ___Yes ___No

EXAMPLES:

_____
_____
_____
_____

Did you keep using after the consequences? _____Yes _____No

EXAMPLES:

_____
_____
_____
_____

Has worthless kept you from other activities? _____Yes _____No

EXAMPLES:

_____
_____
_____
_____

Has worthless absorbed more and more time? _____Yes _____No

EXAMPLES:

_____
_____
_____
_____

Have you been using worthless more and more? _____Yes _____No

EXAMPLES:

_____
_____
_____
_____

> **IF YOU HAVE ANSWERED YES TO SEVERAL OF THESE QUESTIONS, THEN YOU HAVE AN ADDICTION TO WORTHLESS.**
>
> **IDENTIFYING THAT YOU HAVE AN ADDICTION CAN FINALLY GIVE YOU THE ANSWERS TO WHY YOU AREN'T SUCCESSFULLY MOVING PAST WORTHLESSNESS.**

If you believe you have been addicted to worthlessness then we encourage you to do the Steps workbook portion in the back of this workbook. If you don't think you are addicted to worthless, you can skip the Steps workbook portion of this book.

DAY TWO

LESS THAN

A common theme for someone who struggles with worthlessness is how he or she relates to others. A person who feels unworthy will really relate to others from an unequal position of value.

One way that those who struggle with not feeling worthy relate to others is by seeing themselves as "less than" others or in a less-than position compared with others. Here are twelve characteristics of those who manifest a "less than" position around others. If you see yourself in the characteristics below, the worthy process can help you move toward an equal position with others. Place a check next to any statement that you have agreed with in the past.

CHARACTERISTICS OR BELIEFS OF A LESS-THAN POSITION:

- ☐ 1. I feel less-than.
- ☐ 2. My flaws confirm I am less-than.
- ☐ 3. I am to comply with others.
- ☐ 4. I am to second-guess my voice.
- ☐ 5. I can't do anything.
- ☐ 6. Don't try or you will fail.
- ☐ 7. Following is the best position.
- ☐ 8. Saying "no" is difficult.
- ☐ 9. Empathy more important than justice.
- ☐ 10. Question yourself always.
- ☐ 11. Fears opinions of others.
- ☐ 12. I rationalize for others.

I SHARED THIS WITH

# GREATER THAN

There is another position a person can take with others if they feel unworthy. This one may seem counterintuitive, but we all have met this person in our lives.

This person's position toward others is "greater than." They will believe and behave in a way that measures themselves as better than others. Often in this position they feel safe and able to justify the unkind way they treat others. If this has been your position toward others, then the worthy process can help you heal to see, believe, and behave as if everyone has value. Below are the characteristics of the greater-than position. Place a check by any of these statements you have agreed with in the past.

CHARACTERISTICS OF A GREATER-THAN POSITION:

- ☐ 1. I have a greater-than attitude.
- ☐ 2. I have to hide my weaknesses.
- ☐ 3. I comply outwardly.
- ☐ 4. No questions can be asked.
- ☐ 5. I can (outwardly).
- ☐ 6. Try, but don't fail. (Failure is not acceptable.)
- ☐ 7. Leading is more important than following.
- ☐ 8. Justice is more important than empathy.
- ☐ 9. The truth is your perspective.
- ☐ 10. Rationalize your behaviors to others.

I SHARED THIS WITH

DAY THREE
EQUAL TO

As you make progress in receiving, believing, and behaving that you are worthy, you will move away from a less-than position or a greater-than position with others.

You will naturally graduate into seeing yourself as valuable and seeing, believing, and behaving as if others also have significant value. Below are some characteristics of those who come from an equal position toward others. I would like you to acknowledge the statements you currently believe by placing a check by the statement.

CHARACTERISTICS OF AN EQUALLY POSITIONED SOUL:

- ☐ 1. I am equal.
- ☐ 2. I am loved.
- ☐ 3. I am a team player.
- ☐ 4. I have an equal voice.
- ☐ 5. I can do some things well.
- ☐ 6. I can try regardless of results.
- ☐ 7. I can lead or follow.
- ☐ 8. "No" can happen.
- ☐ 9. I can balance justice and empathy.
- ☐ 10. I can question others and myself.
- ☐ 11. I can be fearless.
- ☐ 12. I can apologize when necessary.

THOSE WHO ARE MORE THAN

In my experience, those who struggle with worthlessness have a list of thoughts that regularly bombard their minds. These can also be effects from the enemy in the form of, "You're not...they are."

When we can actually look at the list of characteristics that we often think about, then we can know when this attack is happening. It's time to fight these with the truth that you are worthy, awesome, and complete, and God has made you worthy.

Those who struggle with worthless think that others are more than them for variety of reasons. Which ones apply to you?

WEIGHT   BEAUTY   MONEY   JOB   RELATIONSHIP
INFLUENCE   MINISTRY   EDUCATION

I LEARNED:

_____
_____
_____
_____
_____
_____

I SHARED THIS WITH _____

THOSE WHO YOU THOUGHT WERE WORTH MORE THAN YOU.

1. _____
2. _____
3. _____
4. _____
5. _____
6. _____
7. _____
8. _____
9. _____
10. _____

DAY FOUR
THE OTHER PROBLEM

During my counseling sessions with those who believe and behave as if they are worthless, I have seen another issue come up called Intimacy Anorexia. In marriage, sometimes one spouse has this issue and sometimes both have it.

Intimacy Anorexia is the active withholding of spiritual, emotional, and sexual intimacy from the spouse. The spouse will complain of feeling like a roommate. The characteristics are below. Answer these questions as your spouse would answer these questions—or even better, have them answer these questions directly.

1. I stay so busy that I have little time for my spouse.
2. When issues come up my first reflex or response is to blame my spouse.
3. I withhold love from my spouse.
4. I withhold praise from my spouse.
5. I withhold sex from my spouse or am not fully present during sex.
6. I withhold spiritual connection from my spouse.
7. I am unwilling or unable to share my authentic feelings with my spouse.
8. I use anger or silence to control my spouse.
9. I have ongoing or undergrounded criticism (spoken or unspoken) toward my spouse.
10. I control or shame my spouse regarding money or spending.
11. My spouse had said they feel more like a roommate than a spouse.

If either of you have five or more yes answers, this may be an issue you would like to address on your journey of believing and behaving that you are worthy. If this is the case, then you might want to go to www.IntimacyAnorexia.com for further help with this issue.

I SHARED THIS WITH

DAY FIVE
MENTOR

Your journey toward worthy is moving along now. Let me remind you again that you are worthy of love, respect, honor, and an overall great life.

As you're going through this workbook, I have encouraged you to get support from others. In this exercise I want you to find a mentor who can specifically meet with you face-to-face, through Skype, or over the phone to cover the work that is ahead of you.

This person must be of the same gender, spiritually mature, and believe and behave worthy. This person's role can be as a sounding board, someone to share your thoughts with when needed.

Take a day or so to think through who this person might be. Think of someone who could play this role in your life as you continue on your worthy journey.

I DECIDED TO ASK _____ **TO BE MY WORTHY MENTOR.**

I SHARED THIS WITH _____.

WEEK SIX

Worthlessness And God
(Refer to Disc One, Chapter Six)

FILL OUT DURING DVD SESSION:

1. Worthless says b_____ me.

2. Worthless doesn't want you to believe in God but in w_____.

3. Worthlessness is not coming from G_____.

4. If I made w_____, then I can d_____ worthless.

5. Worthless and God both want to be o_____.

6. As you improve becoming worthy you will improve obeying G_____.

7. Who He is m_____.

8. Believe y_____ o_____ behavior.

9. Our theology is our b_____.

10. Take your f_____ to unquestionably believe your w_____.

11. Faith in G_____ will detract from your faith in worthless!

NOTES:

_____
_____
_____
_____
_____

DAY ONE
WORTHLESSNESS AND GOD

Worthy is the heart of God. Worthless competes with the heart of God. It tells you not to believe you are worthy. Others can believe they are worthy, but you can't believe it for yourself. The goal of worthlessness is to get you to not believe God and to believe you are worthless.

Has worthless kept you from believing in God? If so, how?

_____
_____
_____
_____

God didn't make you worthless. He doesn't make anything that isn't worthwhile. Just the fact that you are made in the image of God means you are worthy.

We in our own mindset, made worthless. We either agreed with the enemy telling us that we are worthless or we crafted it in our own flesh and began to believe that we were worthless. This is a judgement you have made on yourself, it is not from God. The good news is, if you made worthless, you can destroy it.

List several ways you have agreed with the voice of worthless:

1. _____   6. _____
2. _____   7. _____
3. _____   8. _____
4. _____   9. _____
5. _____   10. _____

As you begin to believe you are worthy, you will begin to want to obey God and his heart for you.

"Believe behavior" is a key phrase we use in any growth process. Look at your own behavior. Are you really behaving as if you are worthy?

💬 Look at your current behaviors. Are you living as if you are worthless? If so, how?

_____

_____

PROBLEM/SOLUTIONS

Over the decades of working with thousands of clients you learn a few things. One of the mantras in my practice has been, "When I am the problem I am the solution."

Oftentimes people want to blame someone or something for their choice to believe and behave in a worthless lifestyle. I understand about neglect and having things done to you that you didn't ask for, things that you are *not* responsible for.

You see, when other people are the problem, you have no power to free them or your situation. When you are or I am the problem, then we have 100 percent of the responsibility and power to be the solution in our own life.

As you journey to worthy, you will shed blame and embrace responsibility for being your solution. When you move into taking responsibility for worthless thoughts, beliefs, and behaviors, you can change and grow into worthy thoughts, beliefs, and behaviors.

In the space below write out how you need to become your own solution.

_____

_____

_____

_____

> **QUOTE**
>
> YOU WERE CREATED WORTHWHILE, BELIEVE YOU ARE UNIQUE, BELIEVE YOU ARE TALENTED, BELIEVE YOU ARE IRREPLACEABLE.

I SHARED THIS WITH _____.

I honestly believe that if you can take the faith that God has given you as a child and unquestionably believe you are worthy, you will be UNSTOPPABLE. When you have faith in who God is, instead of in worthless, your faith will function as it was designed to. Your faith in God will detract from your belief in worthless.

List several ways that you can grow your faith in God:

1. _____
2. _____
3. _____
4. _____
5. _____
6. _____
7. _____
8. _____
9. _____
10. _____

STEP THREE

"MADE A DECISION TO TURN OUR LIFE AND WILL OVER TO THE CARE OF GOD AS WE UNDERSTOOD HIM."

Making a decision of this magnitude can and should take some time in your journey toward becoming worthy. In Step Two, we were spending time with God, discovering His existence, and how this relationship is working out. Having a relationship with God is much like falling in love and getting married. First, we dated our spouse. Eventually, over time and experiences, we decided to marry them and followed through with this decision. The decision to marry affected every part of our life socially, financially, sexually, and emotionally. In various other areas, marriage redefined our behaviors and us.

Turning your life over to the care of God is a similar experience. It is walking down the aisle with God and a lifelong commitment to stay in a relationship. This relationship grows over time. The depth of our experience and time together will reinforce our conception of God. As a Christian struggling with worthless beliefs and behaviors, turning your desire over to God will be essential. It will be very important for you to be willing to accept His interpretation of your needs and trust Him to meet them. Turning over your life and your will means you are ready for Him to have total authority over those thoughts of worthlessness. You are willing to start believing with your will that you are worthy.

CHECK OFF THE BEHAVIORS YOU CURRENTLY HAVE THAT SUPPORT YOUR STEP THREE.

Behavior	Yes	No
1. Prayer	___	___
2. Spiritual reading	___	___
3. Asking God to be involved in every area of your life	___	___
4. Behaviorally follow what you know to be God's will, even when you want it another way	___	___

The day I completed my Third Step was _____

DAY TWO
IDENTIFYING AND COMMUNICATING FEELINGS

The majority of people who struggle with worthlessness have difficulty identifying their feelings. Most people have not had any experience within their family of origin at how to have and share feelings. Feelings are a skill you can develop for which you can acquire levels of mastery once you have practiced. For example, when you were growing up you may not have learned how to maintain a car. It doesn't mean you are less intelligent or worthwhile because you cannot fix a car. You are simply untrained. If you were to take a class on car maintenance, you would probably be a good mechanic. The difference is in the skills you were exposed to on your journey to believing that and behaving like you are innately worthy. Here is what this emotional journey can look like.

1. If you had a feeling you probably would not know what it was. If you acted out or ignored it in some way, the feeling would eventually go away. In this process, you may not have learned to identify feelings and, hence, cannot meet your own real needs.

2. As you move in your journey toward feeling worthy you begin to feel again. It will seem almost like a thawing out of emotions. It is best to have actually begun to identify your feelings so they don't confuse or overwhelm you and activate confusion, which could lead to thoughts of worthlessness.

3. If you can identify your feelings, you may better know how to handle or manage these feelings in order to prevent attacks of worthlessness.

4. If you have a worthless attack you may be able to track down what emotion(s) preceded this and move forward in your journey to becoming worthy.

5. Mastering your feelings can allow more intimacy in your life, and, yes, it will make your relationships better too.

In the first month or so of your journey, the feelings-identification exercise may be one of the more difficult exercises in this book. The discipline you put into this exercise will have lifelong benefits in every area of your life, including in relationships, parenting, work, spirituality, and your social life.

The feelings exercise is simple. Fill in the blanks. An example is given below.

1. I feel (<u>feelings word</u>) when _____(present tense)

2. I first remember feeling (<u>same feeling word</u>) when _____ (past tense)

EXAMPLE:

1. I feel <u>calm</u> when <u>I am on the lake in a boat with a friend</u>.

2. I first remember feeling <u>calm</u> when I was ten years old. <u>I had my own bedroom where I played with a racecar set.</u>

The goal here is to have two experiences. In computer terms, we have an emotional database, but this database has no file names, so you cannot access the files, nor can you utilize this data. If you do this exercise two or more times daily for three months, it will make your journey a lot smoother. Those who do this in their journey early never regret it later. Those who do not do this exercise always regret it. I strongly encourage you to take the time to do this exercise today and for the next several weeks.

A feelings list you can utilize for your feeling exercises is located in the appendix of this book. The list is in alphabetical order. You can select any feeling from the feelings list you wish to randomly practice sharing your feelings exercise. If you want to take your emotional skill to a higher level I would recommend my book called *Emotional Fitness*.

FEELINGS COMMUNICATION

When you do this exercise it is important you do it with a safe person. A safe person may be someone in your worthy group or a person to whom you are accountable. The person's role is simply to listen, not really provide feedback. If you choose your spouse, make sure this is safe for you, and <u>*make sure your examples do not involve your spouse in any way.*</u>

If you involve your spouse, they can do the exercise to identify and communicate feelings back to you also. This can be a great opportunity to develop intimacy. If these experiences turn into disagreements, the exercise is being done incorrectly, and you may need to pick another person or a therapist to do them with.

When sharing your feelings, it is important to maintain eye contact with the person you are sharing them with. Eye contact with this person may feel uncomfortable at first but eventually will become comfortable to you. This is part of the benefit of this exercise. If you do them with your spouse, there is to be no discussion of what was shared in this exercise until seventy-two hours after the feeling was shared.

I SHARED THIS WITH

_____

MY E ZONES

Emotions for those on the journey toward worthy can be tricky. Early in the journey, those who struggle with believing and behaving worthless have few feelings skills. In your journey, especially after completing your feelings exercises, you will become better acquainted with yourself and your feelings.

Being aware of your feelings will be helpful, but it will not make them less difficult. In your journey, you will find some feelings are very difficult for you to manage. Some feelings may include, but are not limited to, boredom, loneliness, anger, hopelessness, worthlessness, shame, and rejection.

These difficult feelings are what I call the dangerous *E* zones. They are feelings you have skillfully avoided or medicated, which is what makes them a possible, dangerous *E* zone. They represent a cluster of feelings you rarely have felt without going into a worthless attack.

During your journey, you need to discover your dangerous *E* zones. The easiest way is to review the feelings list and place a mark either by the feelings you believe to be most difficult for you or the feelings that spiral you into a worthless attack.

LIST THESE FEELING WORDS BELOW

_____   _____

_____   _____

_____   _____

_____   _____

EFFECTS

When you are caught in the spiral of believing and behaving worthless, you are, to a degree, consumed with yourself. Like a drug addict or alcoholic, you will have very little insight into how your behavior is actually impacting those you love.

This might be hard to acknowledge because you might spiritualize your worthlessness and believe you're serving that person. But what actually is happening is that you are staying crippled and dependent on yourself. For example, others are in pain as they watch as you self-depreciate or not reach for goals to change your circumstance.

Below is a list of possible relationships that your believing and behaving worthlessly could be impacting negatively. Write down how you think your worthlessness is affecting them:

GOD _____

YOUR PARENTS _____

SPOUSE _____

CHILDREN _____

FRIENDS _____

PARTNER _____

NEIGHBORS _____

SIBLINGS _____

COWORKERS _____

I SHARED THIS WITH

DAY THREE
STEP FOUR

"MADE A SEARCHING AND FEARLESS INVENTORY OF OURSELVES."

Making a personal inventory is helpful in many ways. First, an inventory tells you what has happened and when it happened, both good and harmful. Second, this inventory will give you insight into patterns or cycles of unhealthy behavior.

Without this "spreadsheet" you would not be able to see clearly. There are several ways to complete a Fourth Step but all include, in one way or another, writing it down somewhere.

Let's define a few terms first, such as the word "good," which indicates positive things that have happened. "Bad" will mean things you did that you knew were wrong and did them despite this knowledge. "Ugly" will be things that happened to you that you weren't responsible for, such as car accidents, surgeries, parents' divorce, abuse, or neglect. With these terms in mind, take a piece of paper, draw your columns and a place for the span of years as seen below, and complete "the rest of the story." Below are some examples.

YEARS	GOOD	BAD	UGLY
1-5			
6-10	won spelling bee		Placed in foster home
11-15		stole porn	
16-20.....			

CHECK OFF THE BEHAVIORS YOU CURRENTLY HAVE THAT SUPPORT YOUR STEP FOUR.

Behavior   Yes   No

1. Consistent time spent writing your story   ___   ___
2. Compete honesty on your story   ___   ___
3. Checking in if memories affect sobriety   ___   ___

The day I completed my Fourth Step was _____.

WORTHY: FIVE YEARS FROM NOW

Fighting worthlessness with pictures is an effective way to help you combat the times your worthlessness wants to creep back in. Many times your worthlessness will try to sneak back in through pictures. Worthlessness knows how your brain works and how powerful pictures are. Vivid, reinforced pictures are quickly accessible to the brain's memory.

A helpful picture for combating worthlessness is one in which you are having personal success: enjoying yourself, your marriage, family, career, and other relationships and activities.

As someone who has experienced the positive picture of being worthy and living a happy, fulfilling, and balanced life, I know this picture helps fight off a worthless attack when it wants to sneak its ugly head in. In the space provided below or on a separate sheet of paper, write out what you think your life would be like if you were to maintain worthiness in life.

The following situations could be included in your response:

1. The friends you would have
2. Your career
3. Your marital status
4. Your relationship with your children
5. Your health
6. How you feel about yourself
7. Your spiritual lifestyle
8. Recreational interests or hobbies
9. Anything else you see for yourself in a positive future of being worthy

💬 How my life in recovery will look five years from now:
_____
_____
_____
_____

Take this picture and practice it two or three times a day for three to five days along with the feelings that go with it. This picture can be yours. After the hard work that comes with a healthy worthy lifestyle, there can be fulfillment in every life area: spiritual, emotional, health, marriage, friendship, family, and financial. My hope is you experience this picture. I have experienced it, and I know you can too.

Your feelings about this picture:
_____
_____
_____
_____

I SHARED THIS WITH

DAY FOUR
STEP FIVE

"ADMITTED TO GOD, OURSELVES AND TO ANOTHER HUMAN BEING THE EXACT NATURE OF OUR WRONGS."

In Step Four, you provided yourself with all the information you need to complete Step Five. Step Four is "your" story. It is a story that has shadows, much like others have who are healing from worthlessness. You need to admit this story to yourself, which usually happens during the writing, reading, or sharing of your Fourth Step.

For some, "admitting to God" has been an event all by itself. God already knows, but something can happen when you tell Him where you have been. Some find it helpful to visually put God in an empty chair and read their story to Him. This may be a helpful exercise to do in the process of completing your Fifth Step.

Having "another human being" involved is by far the toughest part. Allowing someone else into your closet of secrets is difficult but entirely necessary for you to have the worthy life. Select a person in your group, a person of the same sex (not your spouse), or a pastor or a therapist to share your story with.

The Fifth Step is a must in your claiming the worthy life. While finishing your Fifth Step, you will feel less guilt and shame and begin to experience acceptance, even though you once believed, "If someone really knew me, they wouldn't love me." This is not true, and in your Fifth Step you will get to experience being human, flaws and all.

CHECK OFF THE BEHAVIORS YOU CURRENTLY HAVE THAT SUPPORT YOUR STEP FIVE.

Behavior	Yes	No
1. A written-down Fourth Step	___	___
2. A time of reflecting with yourself, "admitting to yourself"	___	___
3. A time you and God go through "admitting to yourself"	___	___
4. Picking someone to share your Fifth Step with	___	___
5. Making an appointment to share "your story"	___	___
6. Sharing your story	___	___

The day I completed my Fifth Step was _____.

GRIEF

Worthlessness has probably been your best friend and seemingly only true friend. Quite possibly, it has been there faithfully since adolescence. It has accepted you no matter what hurts you had or what kind of mood you were in any particular day.

When you truly divorce yourself from worthlessness, you will go through a grieving process. This process is normal and healthy. This exercise will help expose you to the stages of grief, so you can understand and identify which stage you find yourself in and discover the future stages ahead of you.

GREIF'S STAGE 1: SHOCK

This is the moment you realized you really were in agreement with worthlessness. Numbness or a sense of emotional nausea may accompany this. This stage is usually fleeting and may last minutes, hours, or sometimes days.

GRIEF'S STAGE 2: DENIAL

This is usually the longest stage of grief. "I don't have a problem," "I am not the problem," "Everyone feels worthless, and depreciates themselves," and "That's just the way I was raised." All of those denials and many others are ways of not looking at worthlessness and not admitting its grip.

GREIF'S STAGE 3: ANGER

This is the first stage in which you begin to process, "I have a problem." You probably will be very angry at this realization. You may dislike that you have been walking in agreement with worthlessness all these decades.

GRIEF'S STAGE 4: BARGAINING

This is the stage when someone might say, "I'm not worthless if..." The *if* can mean, "... if I can stop for a while," or "... if I can just stop one aspect of my behavior." Worthlessness may wish that "if my spouse or life was different, then I would not have this problem." Bargaining seeks to relieve the sting of the fact that you may have actually been in agreement with worthlessness. This is a very creative stage.

GRIEF'S STAGE 5: SORROW

This is when it starts hitting you. You have been believing and behaving in a worthless manner. This may not feel very good, but the realization is true. You know things need to change. You can feel it. You are sad about being in agreement with worthlessness and maybe sad too about what it has done to your life and the lives of those you tried to love.

GRIEF'S STAGE 6: ACCEPTANCE

You are able to say, "I have been walking in agreement with the belief that I was worthless." You now accept responsibility for your beliefs and behaviors related to worthlessness. You are no longer blaming or looking for a magical way to avoid the journey to worthy. Your behavior is active—you are involved in your worthy journey. Your creativity is being used to find time and ways to receive and reclaim your worth; and you are being honest, even when it hurts.

In the space below, circle the stage you believe you currently are in. In a few weeks, check back and see if there is movement from that stage. Grief is a process. Being in grief is okay, because if you pass denial, you are actively going through the reality of moving from a worthless position to a fully worthy position. You can also write about each stage you have experienced.

SHOCK   DENIAL   ANGER   BARGAINING   SORROW   ACCEPTANCE

SHOCK_____

_____

_____

_____

_____

DENIAL_____

_____

_____

_____

_____

ANGER_____

_____

_____

_____

_____

BARGAINING_____

_____

_____

_____

_____

SORROW_____

_____

_____

_____

_____

ACCEPTANCE_____

_____

_____

_____

_____

DAY FIVE
MY FAMILY

I have walked with Christ without addictions for almost thirty years. One of the phenomenal things I have seen is how addictions can run down a family tree. Similarly, those who believe and behave in a worthless manner also can have an addiction to worthlessness or abuse throughout their family tree.

💬 Below I want you to circle those in your extended family who have struggled with worthless lifestyle beliefs or behaviors, been abused, or had addiction issues.

Grandparents (Dad)	Abuse	Addiction	Worthless Lifestyle
Grandparents (Mom)	Abuse	Addiction	Worthless Lifestyle

Dad's Siblings

1.	Abuse	Addiction	Worthless Lifestyle
2.	Abuse	Addiction	Worthless Lifestyle
3.	Abuse	Addiction	Worthless Lifestyle
4.	Abuse	Addiction	Worthless Lifestyle

Mom's Siblings

1.	Abuse	Addiction	Worthless Lifestyle
2.	Abuse	Addiction	Worthless Lifestyle
3.	Abuse	Addiction	Worthless Lifestyle
4.	Abuse	Addiction	Worthless Lifestyle

Dad	Abuse	Addiction	Worthless Lifestyle
Mom	Abuse	Addiction	Worthless Lifestyle
Siblings	Abuse	Addiction	Worthless Lifestyle
1.	Abuse	Addiction	Worthless Lifestyle
2.	Abuse	Addiction	Worthless Lifestyle
3.	Abuse	Addiction	Worthless Lifestyle
4.	Abuse	Addiction	Worthless Lifestyle

Cousins	Abuse	Addiction	Worthless Lifestyle
1.	Abuse	Addiction	Worthless Lifestyle
2.	Abuse	Addiction	Worthless Lifestyle
3.	Abuse	Addiction	Worthless Lifestyle
4.	Abuse	Addiction	Worthless Lifestyle

I SHARED THIS WITH

HISTORY LESSONS

As you contemplate the last exercise, also think about whether there has been a history in your family of abuse, addiction, or a lifestyle of worthlessness. In the space below, write down what you learned from looking at your family tree.

_____
_____
_____
_____
_____
_____
_____
_____
_____
_____
_____
_____
_____
_____
_____
_____

WEEK SEVEN

Being Worthy
(Refer to Disc Two, Chapter One)

FILL OUT DURING DVD SESSION:

1. Being worthy is i_____.

2. You can separate yourself from your w_____.

3. The truth is that you are w_____.

4. You're worthy because He s_____ so.

5. You're worth the g_____ He gave you.

NOTES:

_____
_____
_____
_____
_____
_____
_____
_____
_____

DAY ONE
BEING WORTHY

Being worthy is inate. You were created to be worthy. There is nothing that you can do to not be worthy. He died for you. He loves you. There is nothing that can separate you from your worth, except YOU. You can, in your mind, contradict this. You were given worth the moment you were born. At that moment, God chose to love you.

What do you think about being innately worthy?

_____

_____

(...) What does it mean to you that God Himself believes you are worthy?

_____

_____

The Holy Spirit comes into our lives and gives us an incredible way to communicate with the Father. The Holy Spirit continues to work on our hearts to bring light to things in our lives that can separate us from truly believing our worth. The very fact that the Holy Spirit lives in us declares that you are worthy.

The truth is, You are worthy! Because He says so!

Are you beginning to truly believe this? __Yes __No

From 1 to 10 on the scale below, where would you place yourself as to what you actually believe and how you behave?

(...) **Worthless**   1 2 3 4 5 6 7 8 9 10   **Worthy**
   (My idea)   (God's Truth)

DAY TWO
STEP SIX

"WERE ENTIRELY READY TO HAVE GOD REMOVE ALL THESE DEFECTS OF CHARACTER."

Now that you have written and acknowledged your story to God, yourself, and another person, defects of character may be more obvious to you. In Step Six, you can begin to see some of your limitations—or things about yourself that are less than positive. It has been helpful for many who are on the journey to worthiness, before they can become "entirely ready," to take some reflective time to list their defects of character. Writing down your defects (i.e., "impatient," "manipulative," "selfish") helps you to know what you are preparing to have God remove.

The simplest way to do this is to list in the left column your character defects. Next to the character defect, write the percentage your willingness is for God to remove this defect (i.e., Selfishness, 75%). Review your list regularly until there is a "100%" next to each defect. During the start of this list and its completion, you may want to pray over the areas you are less than 100 percent ready for God to remove.

CHECK OFF THE BEHAVIORS YOU CURRENTLY HAVE THAT SUPPORT YOUR STEP SIX.

Behavior	Yes	No
1. A list of "defects of character"	___	___
2. A regular review until 100% "entirely ready"	___	___
3. Prayer during the process of becoming "entirely ready"	___	___
4. Discussions about defects taking longer to be "entirely ready"	___	___

The day I completed my Sixth Step was _____.

DAY THREE
DATING

Looking back on history allows us to see through a mature lens sometimes less than mature behavior or thinking. People with worthless thoughts and behaviors seem to attract others who are either like-minded or think they are worth more than you are and therefore entitled to treat you in a worthless manner.

It is possible as well that you dated someone who believed you were worth more than you ever thought and consistently treated you with honor and respect. You might have had to reject this person in order to maintain your worthless thoughts, or maybe you grew into this relationship.

On a separate sheet of paper make a list of the people you dated. Evaluate their behavior toward you. Then add some information about how you generally felt in that relationship. See the following example:

John—treated me worthless by……..
   I felt untrusted, unimportant, dumb, etc.

Sally—treated me really well. I pushed her away.
   I felt controlled, called up, ill equipped, etc.

> **THERE IS NOTHING THAT CAN SEPARATE YOU FROM YOUR WORTH, EXCEPT YOU.**

DATING HISTORY

As you went through the previous section about the history of the dating period of your life, you probably had some thoughts, gained some insights, or even discovered some patterns about yourself. Honesty about this can help you to see yourself with honesty in your future.

Write down the thoughts, insights, and patterns you saw:

_____
_____
_____
_____
_____
_____
_____
_____
_____
_____
_____
_____
_____
_____
_____
_____
_____
_____
_____

I SHARED THIS WITH _____.

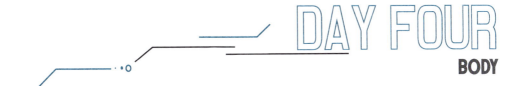

DAY FOUR
BODY

We are so blessed to be created with a magnificent body. Our body is an extension of our amazing Creator: we are made in His image. However, the way we believe and behave can have a significant impact on how we take care of, neglect, or even abuse this magnificent body of ours.

I have heard all kinds of extreme examples—including:

- Not exercising
- Obesity
- Over-exercising
- Not eating healthy
- Not addressing medical issues
- Getting STDs
- Taking unnecessary risks to make someone else happy

You're aware of how you have treated your body in adolescence, young adulthood, and adulthood.

💬 In the space that follows, write out what you believe have been the impacts on your body of your believing and behaving worthless.

_____
_____
_____
_____
_____
_____

SEXUALITY

Your sexuality is a sacred gift your Father in heaven has given to you. In your previous state of believing and behaving, you may have also been less than responsible in your sexuality.

On one hand, you may have experienced sexual trauma, which is no fault of your own; however, it can impact your sexuality. While experiencing worthlessness, you could have engaged in sexuality irresponsibly. You could have participated in abortions in this stage, as well. Some who have engaged in sex acts or viewing pornography may have damaged their sexuality.

Worthlessness can also keep you from being sexually free enough to give all of yourself to your spouse. You may have hang-ups, limitations, avoidance of intimacy during sex, or even avoidance of sex altogether. Or, sexually speaking, you may allow others to treat you poorly or abusively. Worthlessness impacts almost every area of life, including your sexuality.

On a separate sheet of paper write down how you believe your thinking and behaving worthlessly has impacted your sexuality. Include whether you think it has impacted your ability to be fully engaged sexually as well as whether you find yourself tolerating unacceptable sexual behavior.

In the space below write down what you learned in this exercise.

_____
_____
_____
_____
_____
_____
_____
_____
_____
_____

DAY FIVE
SEX EXCHANGE

When counseling women and men who struggle with worthlessness, it can be important to see how they have valued sex. On a separate piece of paper make a list of all the people you have had sex acts with in your life.

Next to their name, write down what you were hoping to get out of the relationship in exchange for your sexuality. This may be very important for seeing what your behavior tells you about what you believed back then—so that you are better informed in your present worthy state. The previous exercise can also help you to identify the type of sex you experienced with each person on your list.

Second, look for any other patterns you can find in the people you had sex acts with. Age, personality, and so on.

In the following space write a summary of what you learned.

_____
_____
_____
_____
_____
_____

WEEK EIGHT

Sense of Worth
(Refer to Disc Two, Chapter Two)

FILL OUT DURING DVD SESSION:

1. Worthy is a gift G_____ gave to you.

2. What two choices do you have with this gift?

    a. I_____

    b. R_____

3. When you are worthy you are r_____ with the gifts God gives to you.

4. When you are responsible you have a sense of i_____ worth.

5. Doing nothing causes d_____.

6. When you know you are worthy, you see your spouse as w_____.

NOTES:

_____
_____
_____
_____
_____
_____
_____
_____
_____
_____

DAY ONE
SENSE OF WORTH

As you move into believing you are worthy, you will have a sense of worthy. It will be a part of who you are. Worthy is a gift God has given to you. You have two choices. You can be responsible or irresponsible with this gift. When you are worthy you are responsible for the things God has given you. When you are responsible you will actually increase your value. You will feel a sense of esteem.

When you believe you are worthy you will automatically take better care of your spouse, your children, your community. When you are responsible, you are responding well.

Read: Matthew 25:14-30

In what ways can you be responsible with the things God has given you?

1. _____
2. _____
3. _____
4. _____
5. _____
6. _____
7. _____
8. _____
9. _____
10. _____

If you are not being responsible who or what have you blamed as the reason for this?

_____
_____
_____
_____
_____
_____
_____

> **QUOTE**
>
> **WORTHY IS A GIFT GOD HAS GIVEN YOU.**

MY MARRIAGE

By now in your journey to worthy you have seen how the worthlessness you agreed with has impacted not only you but also your spouse. More than anyone, your spouse would have been impacted by your thoughts and feelings of worthlessness.

It will take courage to be honest and see how your choice not to love yourself may have limited or otherwise impacted your ability to love your spouse, set boundaries, or encourage your spouse to reach for the stars God has put in his or her heart.

On a separate piece of paper do your best to list how your thoughts and behaviors of worthlessness over the years have impacted your spouse.

In the following space, write a summary of what you learned by doing this exercise.

_____
_____
_____
_____

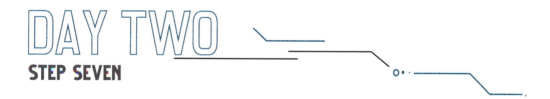

DAY TWO
STEP SEVEN

"HUMBLY ASKED HIM TO REMOVE OUR SHORTCOMINGS."

You may be very familiar with your shortcomings. Being too familiar with your shortcomings can sometimes make it difficult to get into a humble place and ask God to remove them. In my life, my shortcomings hurt those I loved very much. In looking back, these same shortcomings hurt me too. Shortcomings often need a real miracle to be removed.

I liken this process to that of your child, parent, or spouse who might suddenly be diagnosed with a life-threatening disease and all the doctor had to say is, "If you pray, now is a good time to do so." Many of us, regardless of our life history or circumstances, would muster up a "humble-asking" position before God. If someone was watching you, they might call it begging, pleading for God to be merciful "just this once." This is the place to be while completing your Seventh Step.

Asking God to remove your shortcomings is very hard spiritual work. While working on Step Seven, you may want to seriously consider completing just one or two defects a day. More than this may be too draining or may minimize this defect. Some have found it helpful to write down a paragraph or two about how a defect of character has hurt them or others. This will assist in humbly asking God to remove them.

CHECK OFF THE BEHAVIORS YOU CURRENTLY HAVE THAT SUPPORT YOUR STEP SEVEN.

Behavior	Yes	No
1. List of defects	___	___
2. Paragraph of how defects affect you and those you love	___	___
3. A reflective time	___	___
4. A prayer time for each defect	___	___

The day I completed my Seventh Step was _____.

DAY THREE
ABUSE AND NEGLECT

Many who have struggled with believing and behaving in a worthless lifestyle have experienced various forms of abuse. Some emotional abuse could consist of being shamed, degraded, humiliated, or yelled at regularly.

Emotional neglect could involve not being talked to or nurtured, or not having someone care or inquire about how you feel. They may not have inquired about your feelings.

Physical abuse would include hitting or watching others being hit. *Physical neglect* would include being improperly clothed or not having adequate food or shelter.

Spiritual abuse can sometimes mean being emotionally or physically abused while your parents justify this with their religious beliefs.

Some sexual abuse instances would include exposure to pornography, verbal or sexual innuendoes, sexual touches, and other behaviors. Sexual neglect is not informing you about your bodily changes and about sex.

In the space below, check the areas of abuse and/or neglect you feel you have experienced.

ABUSES		NEGLECTS	
Emotional	_____	Emotional	_____
Physical	_____	Physical	_____
Spiritual	_____	Spiritual	_____
Sexual	_____	Sexual	_____

I SHARED THIS WITH

_____.

MY PERPETRATORS

In the previous exercise, you took a look at the abuses and neglects you may have experienced. In this exercise, you are going to look at the people who were responsible for these abuses and neglects.

I know at this point you may be going into very painful territory. So painful, in fact, that many of these issues may be the very pains that were the foundation for worthless in your life; they may be the very reasons that worthless came into your life in the first place. It is very important to your healing process that you look further into the abuses and neglects you suffered.

You may know your perpetrator's name for many of the incidences you have experienced. For some, these events happened in your own home and were done by parents, stepparents, siblings, or extended family. In other cases, there may be a casual relationship that preceded abuse (i.e., with a neighbor, schoolteacher, or another child at school). For some, the person may have been a stranger, and you may not know the perpetrator's name. Maybe it happened only once, and you never saw that person again.

Whatever their name or relationship was to you, these events have been indelibly written into your life. Now it is time to write down your perpetrator's name (if known), relationship (if any), the type of abuse, and their approximate age when the abuse/neglect occurred. You may need a separate sheet of paper to complete this exercise.

NAME	RELATIONSHIP	ABUSE/NEGLECT	AGE

DAY FOUR
WHAT YOU DID TO ME

What you may have experienced from your perpetrator(s) has most likely left you with a lot of pain for possibly many years. This pain is often free floating inside of you. You may rarely or never talk about what exactly happened. Thus, it may remain like an emotional blob of gel that you have not yet crystallized inside.

In your journey toward worthy, it will be important to feel the pain from the abuse or neglect you experienced. Crystalize it as much as possible. It will be very helpful on your journey toward worthy to identify what exactly happened and later process your feelings about these events.

In this exercise, you will do exactly that. Crystalize the memory. In the previous exercise, you wrote down your perpetrators and their general offenses. It is now time to get specific. *On a separate sheet of paper*, list the perpetrator's name at the top of the page. Write down exactly what your perpetrator did in as much detail as you possibly can.

If you have experienced sexual, physical, or other abuses, this will be painful. If you need the support of others, please call to invite them into this healing process with you. If you feel you need professional help at this point, consider a therapist who specializes in this area.

RANKING MY PERPETRATOR(S)

I SHARED THIS WITH

Ranking your perpetrator(s) may seem like an odd thing to do. After all, any abuse, no matter what kind, should never be experienced by anybody. I know this as well as anyone. By ranking your perpetrator(s), you are not trying in any way to minimize the pain each perpetrator has inflicted on your life.

I compare this exercise to the work of a battle surgeon. Every wound a soldier has is painful, and, yet, some wounds will require different levels of procedures, and some wounds may demand more attention than others. We need to outline a plan for surgery, so when you complete your letter and anger work later, your perpetrator(s) will be ranked in order of your perception of who has caused the most damage and pain.

In this exercise, you will need to categorize the perpetrator(s) by ranking the least abusive first and working up to those who caused major traumas, a process that will require more difficult work from you in the exercises ahead. As you begin working on your ranked order, starting with the least traumatic, you will be stronger, more aware of the process, and have a better grasp of what to expect as you move into the higher-ranked traumatic events.

In the previous exercise, where you listed your perpetrator(s), the abuse/neglect, and their age, now write a rank next to their name. Start with Number 1 as the least offending and move up. The most severe will be the highest-ranked abuse.

DAY FIVE
MY PARENTING

This exercise is just for parents. (Nonparents can skip this exercise.) If you have walked in agreement with worthlessness while raising children, then over the years worthlessness may have had an impact on your children, depending on other circumstances and your spouse's level of worthlessness/worthiness.

On a separate sheet of a paper I want you to do a very brave and honest thing. Journal how having worthlessness in your life has affected your parenting and your children.

In the space that follows, write out what you learned from this exercise.

_____
_____
_____
_____
_____
_____
_____
_____

I SHARED THIS WITH

Week Nine

Breaking the Agreement
(Refer to Disc Two, Chapter Three)

1. When I agree with something it can w_____ with me.

2. If you have made an agreement with worthless you have to b_____ the agreement.

2. Did you ask forgiveness for bringing worthless into your life? Y____ N____

3. I prayed the prayer to agree with being worthy. Y____ N____

4. What did you experience in this session?
_____
_____
_____

5. Place the date here that you officially broke your agreement with worthless.
_____

NOTES:
_____
_____
_____
_____
_____
_____
_____
_____

DAY ONE
BREAKING THE AGREEMENT

Read Amos 3:3

How can you see your life becoming different without this agreement to worthless?

_____
_____
_____
_____

How does it feel to be agreeing with God that you are worthy?

_____
_____
_____
_____

...MY RELATIONSHIP WITH DAD ...

In the space provided, describe your relationship with your Dad as you remember it as a child.

_____
_____
_____
_____
_____

In the space provided, describe your relationship with your Dad as you remember it as a teenager.

_____
_____
_____
_____
_____

In the space provided, describe your relationship with your Dad as you remember it as an adult.

_____
_____
_____
_____
_____

I feel happy about my relationship with Dad because_____
_____
_____

I feel sad about my relationship with Dad because_____
_____
_____

I feel mad about my relationship with Dad because_____
_____
_____

My hope for my relationship with Dad is_____
_____
_____

In the space below or on another piece of paper write a letter to your Dad. This letter is for therapeutic purposes only. It is *not* to be sent to him or seen by him unless you discuss it with a support person or therapist. You can express any feelings or situations in your letter.

_____
_____
_____
_____
_____
_____
_____
_____
_____
_____
_____
_____
_____
_____
_____
_____
_____
_____
_____
_____
_____
_____
_____
_____
_____

I SHARED THIS WITH

DAY TWO
DAD CHAIR

Take the "Dear Dad" letter you wrote and sit in a chair with another chair facing you. When you are ready, read your letter to Dad as if he were right in the chair across from you. You may or may not experience a wide variety of feelings during this exercise.

This empty chair exercise can further your sense of expression toward your Dad, as well as give you a sense of confronting past feelings or issues. Having these issues addressed can leave you less vulnerable to believing or behaving in a worthless lifestyle.

To confront some of these family of origin issues, it is not necessary that you actually go visit your parents to drag up all the stuff you have been processing and try to dump it on them in a one-time conversation. Dumping on them doesn't have to occur for you to get better or even to confront the past issues. What you are about to do may also be very difficult and emotional. If you feel you may need support, please do ask someone to be available.

I SHARED THIS WITH

_____

DAY THREE
MY RELATIONSHIP WITH MOM

(•••) In the space provided, describe your relationship with your Mom as you remember it as a child.

_____
_____
_____
_____

In the space provided, describe your relationship with your Mom as you remember it as a teenager.

_____
_____
_____
_____
_____

In the space provided, describe your relationship with your Mom as you remember it as an adult.

_____
_____
_____
_____
_____

I feel happy about my relationship with Mom because_____
_____
_____

I feel sad about my relationship with Mom because_____
_____
_____

I feel mad about my relationship with Mom because_____
_____
_____

My hope for my relationship with Mom is_____
_____
_____

In the space below or on another piece of paper write a letter to your Mom. This letter is for therapeutic purposes only. It is *not* to be sent to her or seen by her unless you discuss it with your pastor or therapist. You can express any feelings or situations in your letter.

_____
_____
_____
_____
_____
_____
_____
_____
_____
_____
_____
_____
_____
_____
_____
_____
_____
_____
_____
_____
_____
_____

I SHARED THIS WITH

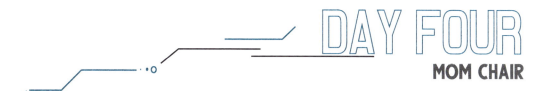

DAY FOUR
MOM CHAIR

Take the "Dear Mom" letter you wrote and sit in a chair with another chair facing you. When you are ready, read your letter to Mom as if she were right in the chair across from you. You may or may not experience a wide variety of feelings during this exercise.

This empty chair exercise can further your sense of expression toward your Mom, as well as give you a sense of confronting past feelings or issues. Having these issues addressed can leave you less vulnerable to believing or behaving in a worthless lifestyle.

To confront some of these family of origin issues, it is not necessary that you actually go visit your parents to drag up all the stuff you have been processing and try to dump it on them in a one-time conversation. Dumping on them doesn't have to occur for you to get better or even to confront the past issues. What you are about to do may also be very difficult and emotional. If you feel you may need support, please do ask someone to be available.

Now you are even further in the worthy lifestyle you deserve and that Christ wants you to experience.

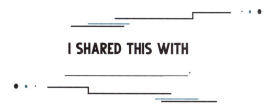

I SHARED THIS WITH

STEP EIGHT

"MADE A LIST OF ALL PERSONS WE HAVE HARMED AND BECAME WILLING TO MAKE AMENDS TO THEM ALL."

Step Eight is yet another that involves journaling. This step is quite straightforward. List on a piece of paper those people you feel you have harmed, especially as it pertains to past believing and behaving as if you were worthless.

In the midst of your past, you were unaware of what you were doing and whom you were hurting. Now, in your journey to worthy, you are sober enough to know your worthless behaviors have a price that needs to be paid. If you need help with this list, consult your fourth Step; most of the people on your "bad" list in that exercise column will qualify for this list in Step Eight.

After you make your list, put a percentage next to it that represents how ready you are at this time to make an amend to this person. For example, Joe, 75%. Review your list regularly until all people on your list have "100%" next to them. This exercise may require your prayers and reflection until all people have a 100% next to their name. Step Eight is meant just to move us to the point we become "willing."

CHECK OFF THE BEHAVIORS YOU CURRENTLY HAVE THAT SUPPORT YOUR STEP EIGHT.

Behavior	Yes	No
1. A list of persons harmed	___	___
2. Percentages that increase	___	___
3. Prayer and Reflection	___	___
4. Discussion with support people over difficult issues	___	___

The day I completed my Eighth Step was _____.

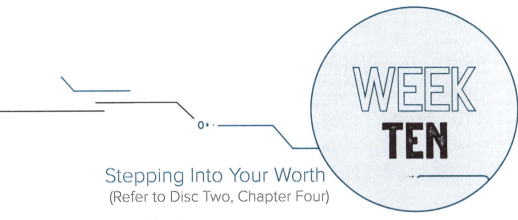

Stepping Into Your Worth
(Refer to Disc Two, Chapter Four)

FILL OUT DURING DVD SESSION:

1. Take step in one a_____ at a time.

2. Have a_____.

3. If we don't confess our faults we are guaranteed to stay s_____.

4. Do your a_____.

5. See your unworthy behaviors and beliefs as s_____.

6. Take r_____ for your talents.

7. You were chosen to be w_____.

NOTES:

_____
_____
_____
_____
_____
_____
_____
_____
_____

DAY ONE
STEPPING INTO YOUR WORTH

List the areas that worthlessness has affected.

1. _____
2. _____
3. _____
4. _____
5. _____
6. _____
7. _____
8. _____
9. _____
10. _____

Accountability is key as you step into your worth. Commit to be honest with another person.

I WILL BE ACCOUNTABLE TO
_____ (NAME)

List your consequence for not stepping into your worth:

_____
_____
_____

DAILY AFFIRMATIONS

In this session, we will be talking about affirmations. You can do your affirmations while lying on your sofa. Relax your body from your feet to the top of your head. Take the list of affirmations (See Appendix) in your hand and read them aloud. You may want to place some of the affirmations on sticky notes and post them where you can see them daily.

💬 In the Appendix you'll see a list of affirmations. Below, I want you to write in the affirmations you will start with.

1._____ 6._____
2._____ 7._____
3._____ 8._____
4._____ 9._____
5._____ 10._____

Below, track your affirmation accomplishments for the first thirty days by circling the days you completed your affirmations.

1 2 3 4 5 6 7 8 9 10 11 12 13 14 15 16
17 18 19 20 21 22 23 24 25 26 27 28 29 30

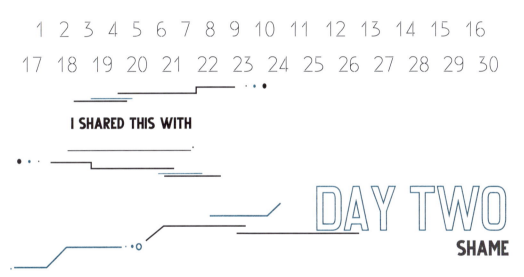

I SHARED THIS WITH _____.

DAY TWO
SHAME

Shame can be one of the primary drivers in someone's life who believes and behaves in a worthless lifestyle. Shame says, "I am bad, ugly, fat, stupid, crazy, or unwanted." Shame wants you to accept a lie about your identity.

Shame removes responsibility for the choices you had in these situations. We all make mistakes in our choices, but that doesn't make us bad. You can easily say, "I make bad choices." This makes two things true: (1) You take responsibility for your choices even if this choice has been made thousands of times over several decades; and (2) When you rephrase "I am bad..." into different choices; you can always make new statements going forward. This is the beauty of being human and loved by God: we innately can change course when we take full responsibility and make new choices.

Shame can also come into your life by the shameful act of another person, such as sexual abuse, physical abuse, rape, or other crimes committed against you. In this case you have taken on their shamefulness as your shame. If you have done your Anger Work and Forgiveness Chair exercises, then this shame is most likely on the way out.

On a separate sheet of paper, write down your "I am" statements about yourself. Almost every person who struggles with worthlessness has "I am" statements. Then write down the "fully accepted responsibility statements" that tell the truth as it is now. Here is an example:

I am worthless:

I made some bad choices. However, I am forgiven for that and I choose to believe Jesus' blood has redeemed those choices. I have accountability now to help me make better choices. I call now when I feel worthless and take responsibility for my behavior or lack thereof.

I SHARED THIS WITH

_____

DAY THREE
I LEARNED

The last exercise was so important that, if you did it, you might have had a paradigm shift from shame to responsibility. In the space that follows, write out a summary of what you learned by doing the last exercise.

_____
_____
_____
_____
_____
_____
_____

_____
_____
_____
_____
_____
_____
_____
_____
_____
_____
_____
_____
_____
_____
_____
_____

I SHARED THIS WITH _____

DAY FOUR
SECRETS

As we continue in our discussion on shame I have to talk about secrets. My experience with shame is that it is often connected to secrets. These secrets tend to fall into two categories.

The first category is things you have done that you are not proud of and haven't told anyone about, ever. I can't tell you how many times clients have told me things they did that they were not proud of. After telling me they felt much better and were able to get free of the shame from that situation.

The second category is things that were done to you that you have never told anyone about. These secrets can also have shame attached to them. Again, when clients told me this type of secret for the first time ever, they were relieved of the shame.

Before you do this with someone, make sure that person is mature and someone who doesn't gossip. If you need to be really safe, see a professional so that your confidentiality is protected. The sooner you accomplish this, the better.

💬 On a separate sheet of paper write down your secrets, or make an appointment to see the person you're going to share this with—and make notes to keep your memory focused because things can get intense.

SHAME LETTER

Many who have had almost a plague of shame in their soul for most of their lives may not even know what it is like to live without shame.

This exercise is something you do *after* you have disclosed your secrets to another person. If you have told someone the secrets that have been plaguing you for decades, you are ready to do these two exercises.

On another piece of paper, write a goodbye letter to shame. Acknowledge its existence in your life, break your agreement with it from your heart, and tell shame an overdue goodbye.

I SHARED THIS WITH

DAY FIVE
STEP NINE

"MADE DIRECT AMENDS TO SUCH PEOPLE WHEREVER POSSIBLE, EXCEPT WHEN TO DO SO WOULD INJURE THEM OR OTHERS."

This step does take into consideration those whom your direct amends *may* injure. This part of the step is not a loophole so that you don't have to make an amend. If you feel you have such a situation, talk with two people who have completed Step Eight and/or a therapist. If they agree with you, then this is probably a legitimate situation for which you should not make an amend. A legitimate example of this would be people you dated and now you are married. Consult your spouse and a therapist before doing this. You can do an empty-chair exercise for those people you were in a romantic/sexual relationship with in the past.

The rest of this step is quite simple to do. With the list you have from Step Eight, write next to each name the most direct approach to do your amend, whether face-to-face, by phone call, or by letter (i.e., Joe, person several states away—phone call). Contacting sexual partners who were part of your past before you married should not be done.

When your list of people and contact methods are complete, you are ready to start. Writing down the date you completed your amend is helpful for keeping you motivated to finish the entire list. A completed entry might look like this.

Joe: Father-in-law   Face to face method   Date completed: 01-12-20

CHECK OFF THE BEHAVIORS YOU CURRENTLY HAVE THAT SUPPORT YOUR STEP NINE.

Behavior	Yes	No
1. A list of people	___	___
2. Method of contact list	___	___
3. Discussion with sponsor or therapist about those you have questions about contacting	___	___
4. Regular progress	___	___
5. A complete list	___	___

The day I completed my Ninth Step was _____.

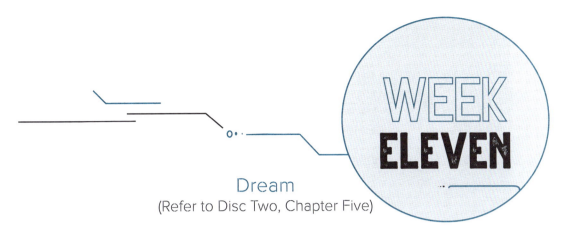

Dream
(Refer to Disc Two, Chapter Five)

FILL OUT DURING DVD SESSION:

1. People with worthlessness often give up on d_____.

2. We tithe because H_____ is worthy.

3. You d_____ to dream.

NOTES:

_____
_____
_____
_____
_____
_____
_____
_____
_____

DAY ONE
DREAM

💬 Write down what your life would look like if you were worthy.

_____
_____
_____
_____
_____
_____
_____
_____
_____
_____
_____
_____
_____
_____
_____
_____
_____
_____

DREAMING RESPONSIBLY

You just wrote down your dream in the last exercise. God has put many dreams in our hearts. Some dreams can take years or even decades to accomplish; however, for a dream to move forward, it needs a few things:

1. You have already written your dream down, which is the first step.

2. Second, share your dream with those most likely to support you in your dream.

3. Third, take steps toward your dream.

4. Next, be accountable to someone as you walk toward your dream.

I will share my dream with _____.

(•••) My action steps toward my dream are as follows:

_____
_____
_____
_____
_____
_____
_____
_____
_____
_____
_____
_____

DAY TWO
FORGIVING YOURSELF

On the journey to worthy we usually have to take a moment, or many moments, in the city of forgiveness. In the city, there may be many citizens you need to forgive. However, the first citizen you need to forgive is yourself.

(•••) Forgiving oneself is important on the journey of worthy. To do this exercise you will need two chairs. In the first chair (A) you will role-play, asking forgiveness of your imaginary self sitting in the other chair (B).

So, I am sitting in chair A and begin talking to Doug, saying: "Doug, I need you to forgive me for…." When I am done asking myself for forgiveness, then I physically move into chair B and respond to Doug's request for forgiveness.

If I do forgive myself, I physically move back to chair A and respond to that forgiveness "Thank you for forgiving me in…." If you are unable to forgive, go back to this exercise one time a month until you do forgive yourself.

FORGIVING OTHERS

Previously you may have made a list of the people who have hurt you or you might still be angry with. In this exercise you will walk through forgiving each person one at a time. You will do this exercise only *after* you have done the anger exercise. Remember, Jesus always cleansed the temple before He said, "Father forgive them."

You will need the two chairs for this exercise. In Chair A, you actually role-play the person who hurt you. Here's an example:

Tony: So, Tony is given a voice through you as if Tony was mature and aware of what he was doing to you.

1. Physically in Chair A, role-play Tony asking you for forgiveness in the other chair.

2. Then switch to Chair B and respond as you would to Tony and be heard here. If you do forgive go back to Chair A (Tony's chair) and respond to you for the forgiveness. If you are not able to forgive Tony, come back to this exercise in a month.

I SHARED THIS WITH

1. You in Chair A asking forgiveness

                                      A   B

2. You in Chair B responding

                                        A   B

3. You responding to the forgiveness or statement

                                        A   B

DAY THREE
WHO I OBEY

When we as Christians get right to the heart of any issue there is a first question that needs to be answered. That question is, who am I obeying?

Worthlessness is a liar and destroyer of your soul. This voice speaks directly to the cross and resurrection of Jesus Christ, who shouts, "You are worthy!"

So when a thought or feeling to act out or believe in a worthless manner comes up as a behavior, you have a choice every time on who you're going to obey: worthless or Jesus. This makes worthless into an obedience issue, not just an issue you struggle with from time to time.

As you walk this journey of worthy, you will be tempted time and time again to obey worthlessness like you have in the past. Jesus has purchased your freedom, but you must claim it.

💬 In the space that follows write out, for yourself, what it means for you that obedience is a choice.

_____
_____
_____
_____
_____
_____
_____
_____
_____

I SHARED THIS WITH

_____

DAY FOUR
TEN THINGS

This exercise is a very simple one. Conceptually, however, it takes quite a while for some people to think through to the point that they include all ten. You see, worthless has you regularly looking at the pimples, or your flaws, instead of at the amazing person whom God has made you to be.

💬 In the space below, write out ten reasons you *love* yourself. I didn't say *like*, or to list things that are just good qualities. I want you to write out ten reasons why you love you!

1. _____
2. _____
3. _____
4. _____
5. _____
6. _____
7. _____
8. _____
9. _____
10. _____

I SHARED THIS WITH

_____.

WHAT BEHAVIORS?

When you fall into the trap of believing you are worthless, it opens you up to behave in words or actions in a worthless manner. Your worthless manifestation will be totally unique. One person overworks; the next person won't get a job; one gains weight; the other is hyper about body image, and so on.

Your manifestations of worthless are important for you to see so you can be healed. As you're on the path to worthy, like the man Jesus asked to stretch forth his withered hand, your worthiness should appear and these behaviors and words should disappear.

In the space below write out ten behaviors you are aware of that have been in agreement with your being worthless.

1. _____
2. _____
3. _____
4. _____
5. _____
6. _____
7. _____
8. _____
9. _____
10. _____

I SHARED THIS WITH

_____.

DAY FIVE
STEP TEN

"CONTINUED TO TAKE PERSONAL INVENTORY AND WHEN WE WERE WRONG, PROMPTLY ADMIT IT."

Continuing to do anything means you have already started doing something. Congratulations! You are entering what some call the "maintenance" part of the Twelve Step process. Step Ten does not allow you to have secrets in your closet, especially now that you put all your time and energy into cleaning it out.

In this step, journaling a daily personal inventory is your tool to make sure you are "staying clean" with yourself and others. In this step, you will reflect daily with yourself and ask the following, "Is there anything I did today that I know wasn't honest or right?" If so, make an amend to this person.

Those who are married or have children will find a lot of opportunities to practice your recovery and stay humble. When this process is integrated, it can provide a lifestyle of honesty for your own well-being and integrity with others.

CHECK OFF THE BEHAVIORS YOU CURRENTLY HAVE THAT SUPPORT YOUR STEP TEN.

Behavior	Yes	No
1. Daily reflection	___	___
2. Check off your findings for the day	___	___
3. Check off daily any offenses made (Remember, "promptly")	___	___
4. Ongoing discussions about steps with sponsor or therapist	___	___

The day I completed my Tenth Step was _____.

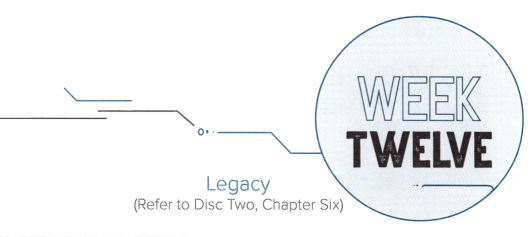

WEEK TWELVE

Legacy
(Refer to Disc Two, Chapter Six)

FILL OUT DURING DVD SESSION:

1. Most of us are part of a legacy of w_____.

2. We are going to leave a l_____.

3. When you are worthy, a_____ all of those around you.

4. God's chosen you to f_____.

5. You want to hear, "Well done, good and f_____ servant.

NOTES:
_____
_____
_____
_____
_____
_____
_____
_____

DAY ONE
WHAT'S NEW?

You have been on your journey of worthy for a while now. You have done many exercises and hopefully had accountability. You have already seen some changes in you behaviors, many from worthless to worthy.

💬 In the spaces that follow write out for yourself ten behaviors you are seeing in yourself that support your new worthy lifestyle.

1. _____
2. _____
3. _____
4. _____
5. _____
6. _____
7. _____
8. _____
9. _____
10. _____

NEW BELIEFS

In the last exercise you wrote down some behaviors that support a worthy you. Now I want you to go deeper with these exercises and list some beliefs that have helped you move from worthlessness to the more worthy you.

1. _____
2. _____
3. _____
4. _____
5. _____

6. _____
7. _____
8. _____
9. _____
10. _____

I SHARED THIS WITH _____.

DAY TWO
BEING CHOSEN

1. In this segment we discussed how God has chosen you to fight. What does it mean to you to be chosen to fight?

   _____
   _____
   _____

2. We also discussed in this segment that each of our heart's desire is to hear the Father say, "Well done good and faithful servant." What will it mean to you to hear the Father say those words to you?

   _____
   _____
   _____

💬 Below, write down what you hope your legacy will be.

_____
_____
_____
_____

OPEN MY HEART

Now that the plague of shame is gone you probably feel different and even a little better. You never have to walk in agreement with shame again. Secrets give shame a right to stay. Once we expose it to the light, we can heal from our shame.

On a separate sheet of paper I want you to write a letter to your heart and give your heart permission to open up all of itself to the love of God.

If you'd like, just sit for a moment and allow the love of God to touch all of your heart. Then write your letter, giving your heart permission to reopen, to open to God, yourself, and others, and to allow the love of God to touch all the places shame was abiding.

In the space below write a summary of your experience.

_____
_____
_____
_____
_____
_____
_____
_____
_____
_____
_____
_____
_____

I SHARED THIS WITH

_____

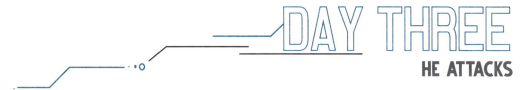

DAY THREE
HE ATTACKS

Here is another biblical principle I learned along the way of helping others. The devil, like any general in an opposing army, wants to stop people from ever attacking him and advancing God's kingdom here on Earth.

So, the reason he attacked you early in your life and throughout your life is because he is scared of you. You in a worthy state carrying your gifts and sword to the battle would be a problem for the devil.

He tries to convince you that you are not worthy. Once you are not worthy, you either won't fight or you won't fight much at all, very hard, or very long. He turns your focus on you instead of the God who restores and commanded you to heal.

Understandably, the devil is scared of you in a worthy state. Knowing this can motivate you to believe and behave in a worthy lifestyle as soon as possible. You are God's plan A on the Earth and there is no plan B.

What do you think about this?

_____
_____
_____
_____
_____
_____
_____
_____

I SHARED THIS WITH

DAY FOUR
STEP ELEVEN

"SOUGHT THROUGH PRAYER AND MEDITATION TO IMPROVE OUR CONSCIOUS CONTACT WITH GOD AS WE UNDERSTAND HIM, PRAYING ONLY FOR THE KNOWLEDGE OF HIS WILL FOR US AND THE POWER TO CARRY THAT OUT."

Prayer has been said to be "talking to God," whether it be requests, petitions, complaints, feelings, or whatever other thoughts you might want to share in your personal relationship with God. Meditation is the point after you have quieted down and actually listen to hear what is on His mind. Both prayer and meditation are important. This is a time to strengthen or improve your relationship with Christ. This is a time of focus spiritually.

Asking God for His will may feel unfamiliar at first, but as you do it, you will realize His will always has your best interest at heart. He is a Father who loves you dearly. Since He takes the time and energy to communicate His will for you, it is my experience that He will give you the power to carry it out. This can open up a whole new aspect to your spiritual life, which will enhance your journey toward worthy.

CHECK OFF THE BEHAVIORS YOU CURRENTLY HAVE THAT SUPPORT YOUR STEP ELEVEN.

Behavior	Yes	No
1. A regular time with God	___	___
2. Journal what God is saying	___	___
3. Keeping track of following God's will and the results	___	___
4. Increased reading and discussing spiritual matters	___	___

The day I completed my Eleventh Step was _____.

DAY FIVE
STEP TWELVE

"HAVING HAD A SPIRITUAL AWAKENING AS A RESULT OF THESE STEPS, WE TRIED TO CARRY THIS MESSAGE TO OTHERS AND TO PRACTICE THESE PRINCIPLES IN ALL OUR AFFAIRS."

I enjoy receiving results, no matter what the activity or area of my life I am working on, especially when the results are obvious. Your recovery has included a lot of hard emotional work and self-discovery. It is through these steps that you had a "spiritual awakening."

You now have something to share. You were believing and behaving in a worthless lifestyle, damaging others and yourself. Now, through this process, you are living a worthy lifestyle, and for the first time, you are able to look at others and yourself. There are people throughout your life who will need this message of hope. When these people come across your path, through whatever circumstances, share your strength, hope, and experience with them.

To be able to believe and behave in a worthy lifestyle is a gift, which the grace of God and your hard work has given to you. To stay worthy is to keep practicing what you learned in your steps and the exercises in this workbook, which has given you a lifestyle of being worthy.

CHECK OFF THE BEHAVIORS YOU CURRENTLY HAVE THAT SUPPORT YOUR STEP TWELVE.

Behavior	Yes	No
1. Continued abstinence from acting out	___	___
2. Continued honesty and integrity	___	___
3. Continued amends when they are due	___	___
4. A lifestyle of healthy relationships	___	___

The day I completed my Twelfth Step was _____.

God has chosen you to leave a legacy of worthy that can changes peoples lives. At the core of who you are, believe that you are worthy! Keep fighting to leave this legacy. So that one day you can hear, "Well done good and faithful servant."

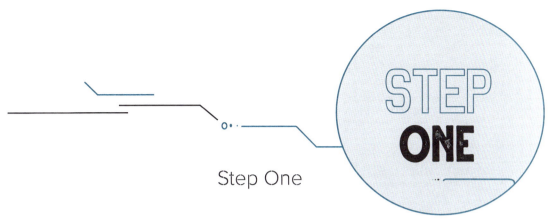

Step One

"WE ADMITTED WE WERE POWERLESS OVER WORTHLESSNESS—THAT OUR LIVES HAD BECOME UNMANAGEABLE."

WE

When asked how to pray, Jesus said, "Our Father." Jesus understood the need for us to have a corporate vision rather than an individual perspective of God. When the apostle Paul wrote the "one anothers" (Gal. 5:13, Col. 3:12-13), he understood the need that believers have for each another. Jesus' brother James also understood this when he penned James 5:16, "Confess your faults *one to another,* and pray *one for another,* that ye may be healed".

There is healing and spiritual power available as you follow the "we" principle in your life. This is especially true as you take the journey through your recovery from worthlessness. In recovery, "we" is a new concept. As a group, "we" can do a lot more than what can be done alone. Especially if you have believed you're worthless. Together "we" can heal. When we are left alone it seems we often stay locked into our worthless thoughts and behavior. We have tried healing by ourselves with little success, but we can heal together.

"We" is one of the most important words that this twelve-step recovery program has to offer. It is in admitting to ourselves that we are powerless over our worthless thoughts and behaviors and need this new "we group" that we can stay free by believing and behaving worthy.

What are some of the first words that come to your mind when you hear the word "we"?

1._____   2._____   3._____

What would you hope to gain from a group healing toward being worthy?

1._____ 3._____

2._____ 4._____

The concept of "we" can be especially hard for people who feel they are worthless because many have lived so much of their lives isolating themselves and their behaviors from others. When you come into a group you will experience that "we" is really obtainable. There are other people who struggle with the same worthless beliefs and behaviors as you.

What are some of the strengths you can see this "we" group adding to your healing from worthlessness?

1._____ 3._____

2._____ 4._____

What are some of the struggles you anticipate when opening up to a group, being honest about your worthless behavior, and letting them support you?

1._____

2._____

3._____

ADMITTED

"Admitted" means to acknowledge what already is a fact. In your case it's often the beliefs or behaviors of being worthless. We need to admit before we can become and stay free and worthy. In Step One, what are you trying to admit to yourself that is probably already a known fact to others?

1._____

2._____

3._____

Who else possibly already knows this fact?

1._____

2._____

3._____

4._____

How do they already know what you are admitting about yourself? (For each person listed, give examples of how they may already know about your worthlessness.)

1._____
2._____
3._____
4._____
5._____

Until now, what has kept you from admitting to yourself that you have believed or behaved worthlessly?

1._____
2._____
3._____

How long have you believed or acted in these worthless ways?_____

POWERLESS

Powerlessness is a state of being that many people do not really accept or even acknowledge. Sometimes we do not face our powerlessness even in the presence of overwhelming facts.

What are some of the facts that lead you to believe that you are powerless over your worthless feelings or behaviors?

1._____
2._____
3._____
4._____

Name people who will try to convince you that you do not need to heal from believing or behaving worthlessly.

1._____   3._____
2._____   4._____

How do you intend to respond to those who will try to convince you that you do not need to address the worthlessness in your life?

1._____
2._____
3._____
4._____

What four behaviors demonstrate that you are presently powerless over your worthless beliefs or behaviors?

1._____   3._____
2._____   4._____

If you are unable to list four behavior patterns that presently reflect your powerlessness, why do you believe you are powerless over your worthless beliefs or behaviors?

_____
_____

What benefits do you see in being powerless over your worthless beliefs or behaviors?

1._____
2._____
3._____
4._____
5._____

How is being powerless over your worthless beliefs or behaviors going to affect the boundaries you set for yourself?

1._____
2._____
3._____
4._____
5._____

How is being powerless over your worthless beliefs or behaviors going to affect friendships or other relationships?

1._____ 3._____

2._____ 4._____

What are other words that describe powerless to you?

1._____ 3._____

2._____ 4._____

How is being powerless over your worthless beliefs or behaviors going to change the activities in your life?

1._____ 3._____

2._____ 4._____

UNMANAGEABLE

"Unmanageable" is another word we often do not like to hear in our culture. We pride ourselves on being in control. List ways your believing or behaving in a worthless manner made you lose control in the following areas of your life:

Spiritual Life

1._____

2._____

Family relationships

1._____

2._____

Financial areas

1._____

2._____

Friendships

1._____

2._____

Relationship with yourself

1._____
2._____

Your Future

1._____
2._____

Vocationally

1._____
2._____

Your Spouse

1._____
2._____

Give examples of when you were unmanageable in your worthless beliefs or behaviors. (Be as specific as possible.)

1._____
2._____
3._____
4._____
5._____

What have your worthless beliefs or behaviors cost you? (Other than money.)

1._____
2._____
3._____
4._____
5._____

How do you feel about your worthless beliefs or behaviors costing others pain?

I feel _____.

I feel _____.

I feel _____.

Why do you want to be free from your worthless beliefs or behaviors?

1._____

2._____

3._____

Do you feel you were truthful while completing this step? Why or why not?

_____

_____

Could you build a new future from the work you have done during Step One? Why?

_____

_____

_____

What is the most significant thing you have learned about yourself during this Step?

_____

_____

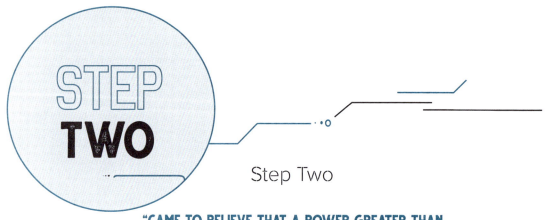

Step Two

"CAME TO BELIEVE THAT A POWER GREATER THAN OURSELVES COULD RESTORE US TO SANITY."

CAME

The verb "came" in Step Two is in the past tense. This word implies the action has already happened. This means that in this Step we are receiving a report of a past event. Highlight in the following spaces examples of God's grace and how He revealed Himself to you when you became a believer in Jesus Christ as your Lord and Savior (i.e., being witnessed to, exposed to Christian events, etc.):

1. _____
2. _____
3. _____
4. _____

Now list some events when the Holy Spirit was trying to share with you that you were worthy of God's love.

1. _____   3. _____
2. _____   4. _____

BELIEVE

To believe is to grow or change. What areas of personal growth have occurred since you came to believe in Jesus Christ as your Lord and Savior? List them in the following space:

1. _____
2. _____
3. _____
4. _____

A POWER GREATER

The phrase "A Power Greater" was the only change of wording in the Twelve Steps from its original writing. The first writing of the Twelve Steps, which began in an Oxford Bible study and birthed Alcoholics Anonymous, read "God" instead of "A Power Greater." The change was made because of the stigma that alcoholics had in the 1930s. To be an alcoholic was very shaming at that time in history. For the alcoholic to go to "God" with his shame was very difficult, so the writers of the Twelve Steps inserted the phrase "A Power Greater" instead, intending to give the alcoholic a little time to develop a God concept. The support groups allow God to patiently reveal Himself to them. Christians can begin to use Christ on their road to worthy. Bringing Christ into your restoration is also a process.

Give specific examples of coming to a point of belief in Jesus in different areas of your life.

1. _____
2. _____
3. _____

What were the results of your faith in these areas of your life?

1. _____
2. _____
3. _____

How has your coming to Christ affected your attitudes about worthless beliefs or behaviors?

_____
_____

When did you come to believe in Jesus Christ? (Approximate date)_____

What happened exactly?

_____
_____

How would you define "greater"?
_____
_____

How do you understand the word or concept of "power"?
_____
_____
_____

What characteristics of Jesus Christ do you believe in?

1._____   4._____
2._____   5._____
3._____   6._____

How do you intend to utilize this relationship with Jesus Christ in your recovery from worthless beliefs or behaviors?
_____
_____
_____

Explain your current relationship with Jesus Christ. _____
_____
_____

What activities or behaviors are involved in your relationship with Him?

1._____   4._____
2._____   5._____
3._____   6._____

COULD

What does it mean to you to believe that Jesus Christ could do something to influence your worthless beliefs or behaviors?
_____
_____

In what ways do you see Jesus Christ becoming involved in your worthless beliefs or behaviors?

1. _____
2. _____
3. _____
4. _____

RESTORE

What does the word "restore" mean to you? _____
_____

In what ways would Jesus have to restore you in the following areas of your life because of your previous beliefs about and behaviors of worthlessness?

Spiritually_____
_____

Fun_____
_____

Parenting_____
_____

Financially_____
_____

Sexually_____
_____

Friendships_____
_____

Realtionship with yourself_____
_____

Marriage_____
_____

What is the most significant thing you have learned about yourself during this Step?
_____
_____

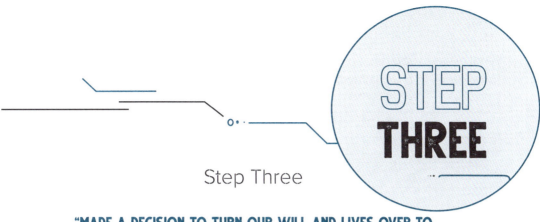

Step Three

"MADE A DECISION TO TURN OUR WILL AND LIVES OVER TO THE CARE OF GOD AS WE UNDERSTOOD HIM."

MADE

Made is the past tense of the verb "to make." *Make* can be defined as "a process involving effort to build or construct something." There are processes involved in making a decision. What are some of the events that have brought you to the point of deciding to turn your life and will over to God?

1. _____
2. _____
3. _____

In the past, you turned your will and life over to various things, persons, or worthless beliefs. List the things, persons, or beliefs you turned your will and life over to in the past. Be specific.

1. _____   3. _____
2. _____   4. _____

Have you had moments of desperation, when you cried out to God to take these worthless beliefs or behaviors away from you? List them.

1. _____   3. _____
2. _____   4. _____

Since the word "made" is in the past tense, explain how you have been affected since turning your will and life over to the care of God, especially as it relates to your worthless beliefs or behaviors. What has changed? What are you doing differently?

_____

What areas in your life are you most reluctant to allow God to be in charge of? List these areas and explain why.

1._____ 1._____
2._____ 2._____
3._____ 3._____
4._____ 4._____

Explain how you will allow God to have His will in these areas.

_____
_____
_____
_____

Over what specific behaviors in your life do you want God to be in charge?

1._____ 3._____
2._____ 4._____

How do you intend to give Him charge over these behaviors?

_____
_____
_____

How are you turning over to God your willingness to act out these worthless beliefs or behaviors?

_____
_____
_____

When did you turn over your will to God? Since then, how have you been behaving differently?

_____
_____
_____

CARE

What other words come to mind when you hear the word "care" as it pertains to the "care of God?"

1._____   3._____
2._____   4._____

How has God cared for you since you have given your will and life to Him?

_____
_____
_____

Had God demonstrated His care for you before you made this decision? If so, list three times.

1._____
2._____
3._____

GOD

God can sometimes be a scary reality to those on the road away from worthless beliefs or behaviors. Especially since His love is against every worthless thought and behavior you have created. On this page, explain God as you understand Him.

_____
_____
_____
_____
_____
_____
_____
_____

What are characteristics you like and dislike about God?

LIKE	**DISLIKE**
1._____	1._____
2._____	2._____
3._____	3._____
4._____	4._____
5._____	5._____

Does God have the freedom to be the final authority in the following areas?

Socially	Yes	No	Job	Yes	No
Financially	Yes	No	Parenting	Yes	No
Marriage	Yes	No	Recovery	Yes	No
Dating	Yes	No	Spiritually	Yes	No
Sexually	Yes	No	Other Addictions	Yes	No

Why do you trust God with your will and life?_____
_____
_____

What do you consider to be your will?_____
_____
_____

What do you consider to be your life?_____
_____
_____

What percentage are you turning over and why? _____

Will _____%   Life _____%

AS WE UNDERSTOOD HIM

We all can learn more about God through prayer, reading the Bible, regular church involvement, and support groups. Ask four people who are spiritually mature to describe God "as they understand Him," as He is active in their lives now.

Record their responses:

1._____
2._____
3._____
4._____

How do you currently practice learning more about God?

1._____   3._____
2._____   4._____

On this page, write a letter to God turning your life and will over to Him.

_____
_____
_____
_____
_____
_____
_____
_____
_____
_____
_____
_____
_____
_____
_____
_____
_____
_____
_____
_____

What is the most significant thing you have learned about yourself in doing your Step Three?

_____
_____

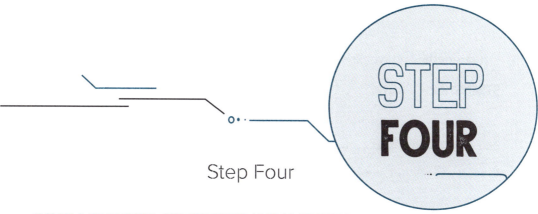

Step Four

"MADE A SEARCHING AND FEARLESS MORAL INVENTORY OF OURSELVES."

MADE

By the end of Step Four we will have made (past tense) a moral inventory of ourselves. Many people struggling with worthless beliefs or behaviors in the midst of their faith did not have the clarity of mind to distinguish between moral or immoral behavior. It is now necessary to do so, lest the guilt or grandiosity pulls you back into your worthless beliefs or behaviors. List strengths and weaknesses you may have in the following areas of your life:

List strengths and weaknesses you have in the spiritual areas of your life:

STRENGTHS	**WEAKNESSES**
1._____	1._____
2._____	2._____
3._____	3._____
4._____	4._____

List strengths and weaknesses you have in the financial areas of your life:

STRENGTHS	**WEAKNESSES**
1._____	1._____
2._____	2._____
3._____	3._____
4._____	4._____

List strengths and weaknesses you have in your relationships:

STRENGTHS
1._____
2._____
3._____
4._____

WEAKNESSES
1._____
2._____
3._____
4._____

List strengths and weaknesses you have in your marital relationship:

STRENGTHS
1._____
2._____
3._____
4._____

WEAKNESSES
1._____
2._____
3._____
4._____

List strengths and weaknesses you have in your vocation:

STRENGTHS
1._____
2._____
3._____
4._____

WEAKNESSES
1._____
2._____
3._____
4._____

List strengths and weaknesses you have had in relating to yourself:

STRENGTHS
1._____
2._____
3._____
4._____

WEAKNESSES
1._____
2._____
3._____
4._____

List strengths and weaknesses you have had in relating sexually with your spouse:

STRENGTHS
1._____

WEAKNESSES
1._____

2._____ 2._____
3._____ 3._____
4._____ 4._____

The above assessment provides an idea of how positive or negative your behaviors have been toward yourself and others. There is yet another inventory to fearlessly take in this step. It is a deliberate search for additional moral information about you.

You will need to be alert as you look at strengths, shortcomings, or losses you have had up to this point in your life. These losses may not have been intentional but have nevertheless caused losses toward others. You may have suffered a loss of innocence from sexual abuse or from sexually abusing others.

LOSSES

Inventory your losses in one column, including harm that was done to you or harm that you may have caused others. This could include abuse (physical, sexual, emotional), divorce, extramarital affairs, death of a loved one, abandonment by a parent, school or legal issues, sexual activity, or other significant events.

In another column list positive occurrences such as school events, career advancements, marriage, and the birth of children. Be specific. Include what happened, with whom, and your feelings then and now about the event. You may want to use a separate sheet of paper to do this part of Step Four.

Ages 1-6

LOSSES   **STRENGTHS**

_____   _____
_____   _____
_____   _____

Ages 7-12

LOSSES   **STRENGTHS**

_____   _____
_____   _____
_____   _____

Ages 13-15

LOSSES

_____
_____
_____

STRENGTHS

_____
_____
_____

Ages 16-25

LOSSES

_____
_____
_____

STRENGTHS

_____
_____
_____

Ages 26-35

LOSSES

_____
_____
_____

STRENGTHS

_____
_____
_____

Ages 36-45

LOSSES

_____
_____
_____

STRENGTHS

_____
_____
_____

Ages 46-55

LOSSES

_____
_____
_____

STRENGTHS

_____
_____
_____

Ages 56-65

LOSSES

_____
_____
_____

STRENGTHS

_____
_____
_____

Age 66 or older

LOSSES	**STRENGTHS**
_____	_____
_____	_____
_____	_____

Have you been 100 percent honest in writing down the losses that you are aware of?

        Yes _____   No _____

Are there specific things you were too ashamed to write down at this point?

        Yes _____   No _____

OURSELVES

The recovering community can help us learn much about ourselves. Contact four recovering people who have completed Step Four and ask what they learned about themselves during this step. Record their first name and answers.

1. _____
2. _____
3. _____
4. _____

What have you learned in this step about the word "ourselves"?

_____
_____

What is the most significant thing you have learned about yourself in completing your Step Four?

_____
_____

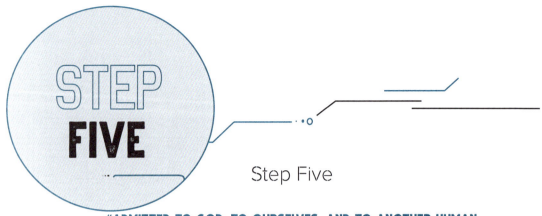

Step Five

"ADMITTED TO GOD, TO OURSELVES, AND TO ANOTHER HUMAN BEING THE EXACT NATURE OF OUR WRONGS."

So far in your journey you have been either reunited, or for the first time, introduced to Jesus. This will help you to admit to Him the exact nature of your wrongs. The journey through Step Four gave you some awareness of yourself. Step Five will further aid you in this understanding.

ADMITTING

Admitting can often be the hardest thing to do. Are there reasons you would like not to entirely admit the exact nature of your wrongs? (i.e., fear of being rejected if others knew?) List these.

1._____   3._____
2._____   4._____

Now we come to an hour of reckoning. Often, to our own harm, as with someone with worthless beliefs or behaviors, we continuously carry a list of things we have done wrong. It is now time to write this list on paper. Make a list of people you are aware of that you have wronged and what their relationship is to you.

NAME	RELATIONSHIP
_____	_____
_____	_____
_____	_____
_____	_____
_____	_____
_____	_____

Write exactly what you did wrong to each of them. Remember to list exactly each wrong done. Use additional paper if necessary.

NAME	WRONG DONE
_____	_____
_____	_____
_____	_____
_____	_____
_____	_____
_____	_____

Now that you have looked at your wrongs from a relational point of view, it is time to look at them chronologically. On the following pages, write the names of those you have wronged physically, sexually, emotionally, and so on, and list them in chronological order of when the wrong was committed. Use your Step Four to help you in this process.

In the space provided, list names of people wronged and a brief explanation of the exact wrong. Include those on previous pages.

Ages 1-6

_____   _____

_____   _____

Ages 7-12

_____   _____

_____   _____

_____   _____

_____   _____

Ages 13-15

_____   _____

_____   _____

_____   _____

_____   _____

Ages 16-25

Ages 26-35

Ages 36-45

Ages 46-55

Ages 56-65

Age 66 or older

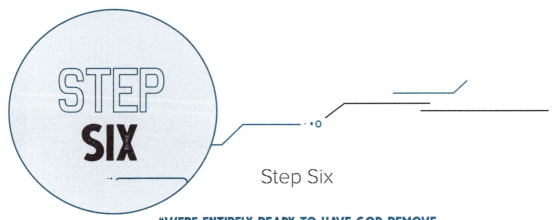

Step Six

"WERE ENTIRELY READY TO HAVE GOD REMOVE ALL THESE DEFECTS OF CHARACTER."

ENTIRELY

When we think of the word "entirely," many pictures come to mind. One of the most vivid pictures is that of a sprint runner who has his foot on the block and hands in the dirt in front of the white line while listening for the gun that is about to go off and signal the start of the race. This is an appropriate picture for "entirely." Entirely is 100 percent ready to do something. Many people with worthless beliefs or behaviors have in the midst of their worthlessness been entirely ready to destroy themselves for the high, the fix, the relationship, or the avoidance of pain from the past.

Now you have come to another point in your life where you need to be entirely ready, after completing Steps One through Five, to do something to better yourself.

What are some of the words you think of when you think of the word "entirely"?

1._____ 3._____

2._____ 4._____

What are some of the feelings you have when you think of the word "entirely"?

I feel _____. I feel _____.

What are a couple of examples in your life when you were entirely ready to do something? (Be specific.)

_____

_____

_____

TO HAVE GOD (JESUS)

Who has Jesus become to you during your journey through Steps One to Five?
_____
_____
_____

What role is He filling in your life?
_____
_____

What feelings do you have toward Jesus at this point?
_____
_____

What aspects or characteristics of God are you relying upon to help in the process of removing your defects of character?
_____
_____
_____

REMOVE

"Remove" is another word in recovery that can mean something very painful for a person with worthless beliefs or behaviors. An analogy of "remove" could be to remove weeds from your grass by pulling them up. Another picture could be to remove a tumor that in the future would have killed you.

What are some of the words you think of when you think of the word "remove"?

1. _____   3. _____
2. _____   4. _____

What are some of the feelings you have when you think of something being removed from you?

I feel _____.   I feel _____.

What are some of the things that have been removed from you up to this point in your healing from worthless beliefs or behaviors?

1._____ 3._____

2._____ 4._____

How has God been involved in the removal process?

_____

_____

ALL

The word "all" means quite a bit to anyone on the road to worthy. It is going to mean a lot also in Step Six. What are some words that come to your mind when you think of the word "all"?

1._____ 3._____

2._____ 4._____

What percentage is "all"? _____%

What percentage do you want all to mean when you talk about removing your defects of character? _____%

DEFECTS

Defects basically are shortcomings or flaws. Having defects doesn't mean we are any less lovable or less human. Diamonds are perhaps the most precious gemstone on Earth. Yet no matter how valuable, big, or rare a diamond is, it has carbon spots (defects) in it somewhere. Like the diamond, we all are going to have carbon spots in our life. This is part of being human. It is not something to be ashamed about, nor is it something to be proud about. However, it is something we can accept and, at this point, identify for ourselves.

What are some of the defects that you have seen in your past?

Ages 1-20

1._____ 5._____

2._____ 6._____

3._____ 7._____

4._____ 8._____

Ages 21-30

1. _____
2. _____
3. _____
4. _____
5. _____
6. _____
7. _____
8. _____

Ages 31-40

1. _____
2. _____
3. _____
4. _____
5. _____
6. _____
7. _____
8. _____

Ages 41-50

1. _____
2. _____
3. _____
4. _____
5. _____
6. _____
7. _____
8. _____

Age 51 or older

1. _____
2. _____
3. _____
4. _____
5. _____
6. _____
7. _____
8. _____

What are some of the defects you have in relating to the following people in your life?

Yourself

1. _____
2. _____
3. _____
4. _____

Your family of origin (parents)

1. _____
2. _____
3. _____
4. _____

Your spouse

1. _____ 3. _____

2. _____ 4. _____

Your children

1. _____ 3. _____

2. _____ 4. _____

Your employer

1. _____ 3. _____

2. _____ 4. _____

Your spiritual authorities

1. _____ 3. _____

2. _____ 4. _____

Your friends

1. _____ 3. _____

2. _____ 4. _____

Your Lord

1. _____ 3. _____

2. _____ 4. _____

Below, compile a full list of these defects of character, the length of time you have been aware of their existence, and the percentage at this point that you are willing to have them removed. An example is given below.

DEFECTS	LENGTH OF TIME	PERCENTAGE
Example: Self-willed	32 years	80-90%

Set some time aside for each one of these character defects and write a paragraph on what your life would be like without this defect in your life. Use the below lines to summarize your writings.

_____
_____
_____
_____

Write in the spaces that follow the character defects that you are 100 percent ready to have God remove. This list would include the character defects that, if God would take them from you, you would let Him have them and not want to take them back.

_____	_____	_____
_____	_____	_____
_____	_____	_____
_____	_____	_____

After a time of prayer and meditation regarding your character defects, write the date below that you became entirely ready for Him to remove all the defects.
_____/_____/_____

CHARACTER

Character is what we are as a person. As we discussed before, there are carbon spots, and these spots are important for us to identify. If we know where the spots are, we can surely ask God to help us with them.

This ends our journey on Step Six. Step Six requests that we become entirely ready to have God remove all our defects of character. So far we have listed our defects and have thought through what it would be like to have them removed.

What is the most significant thing you have learned about yourself in completing Step Six?

_____
_____

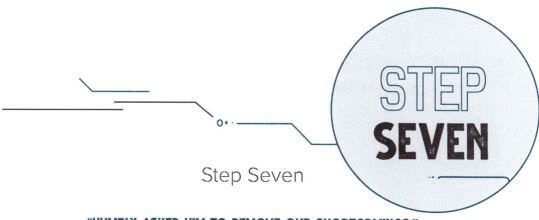

Step Seven

"HUMBLY ASKED HIM TO REMOVE OUR SHORTCOMINGS."

HUMBLY

Humbly can mean a disposition, an attitude, a reverence, or submissiveness. I can remember a couple of past educational experiences in which I was called into the principal's office. I would have what appeared to be a feeling of humbleness while waiting to go into his office. What I was feeling was a knowing that this person could impact my life. An authority figure can have an effect on us; he or she has the authority to do something that affects us either positively or negatively, and we are at that person's disposal. Many of you have experienced something similar to this in your lives at some point. The Scriptures are very clear about the virtue of humbleness in Colossians 3:12, James 4:7-10, and I Peter 5:5-6.

What are some of the experiences you have had that caused you to feel humble?

1._____
2._____
3._____

What are the feelings that accompanied you in those experiences when you were humbled?

I felt _____.   I felt _____.

When was the last time you were in an experience like that?

_____

ASKED

There is an old saying, "You have not because you asked not." This is also true as it relates to our healing in Step Seven. Many people struggling with worthless beliefs or behaviors have never honestly looked at their character defects or limitations. On the following pages we will search further into the meaning of "asked."

What are some of the things that you have asked of God before and you have received them?

1._____
2._____
3._____

Many times it takes faith, trust, or even hope in asking. Some have felt so desperate and full of despair because of shortcomings in their past or current life that they feel as if there is no way out. Now we come to a point where we can ask. Asking doesn't always mean it is going to happen the way we want it to. Nor does it mean that we are going to be in control of the procedure. But let's look at the possibility of asking.

What are some of the things in this step that you would like to ask for?

1._____ 6._____
2._____ 7._____
3._____ 8._____
4._____ 9._____
5._____ 10._____

HIM

What are some aspects of God you are clinging to as you ask Him to do these things for you?

_____

_____

Have you experienced these characteristics before in your relationship with God? If so, how?

1._____
2._____
3._____
4._____
5._____

REMOVE

We talked about the word "remove" in Step Six. This is when we ask for it to actually happen. We are beyond "entirely ready." An analogy of this removal process would be similar to being on a physician's table asking Him to cut into us and remove the cancer that ails us. We are now asking Him to cut deep into our mind and our own will and remove something. During this surgical procedure, you could have a variety of experiences.

Have you had an experience with God removing anything else in your life?

Yes _____ No _____

If so, explain what and how He removed it.

_____

_____

Did you believe that He would do the removal the way He did?

Yes _____ No _____

It is true that the removal process is somewhat of a mystery. Who would think that to create patience you would need to experience situations that would cause you to become patient? Who would think that in the process of becoming kind, you would have to actually change or behave in a different way?

Many of the processes that God is going to use in our lives are not within our control, nor should they be. The removing is not our doing. It is clear that we are asking someone else to do something, much like our asking a surgeon to fix something. We don't have the insight or the education that these surgeons have, nor would many of us want it. We just have to trust that they can do what we are asking them to do.

Have you seen God remove things in other people's lives? Yes _____ No _____

Was he successful in these surgeries? Yes _____ No _____

What are some of your feelings about God being in control of removing the things you listed in Step Six as 100 percent ready for Him to remove?

I feel _____.   I feel _____.

OUR

The word "our" is one of the great words of the Twelve Steps. It means that there is more than just one person who has gone through this. You are not alone, nor will you ever be.

Who are some of the people you know who have done their Step Seven?

1. _____   3. _____

2. _____   4. _____

SHORTCOMINGS

Shortcomings are similar to defects. They are the carbon spots or issues identified in Step Six. Review your Step Six and look carefully over the character defects you identified as being 100 percent ready to have God remove. Write out your prayer to God to remove one character defect at a time. Don't rob yourself and try to clump them all together. Ask Him to take His knowledge and ways to systematically remove them, and give Him full permission to rank them in the order He sees most important and viable. It is much like surgery. Sometimes the surgeon has to prioritize what is going on within the system. If someone has been shot, the surgeon has to look past something else to get at what is primary. Allow God to prioritize as He removes these aspects.

Write down in the spaces provided the list of defects that you have already prayed about. In one year, come back to this and see how much work God has done.

DEFECTS	DATE PRAYED	MY ONE-YEAR PROGRESS NOTE FOR REMOVAL

What is the most significant thing you've learned about yourself while completing Step Seven?

_____

_____

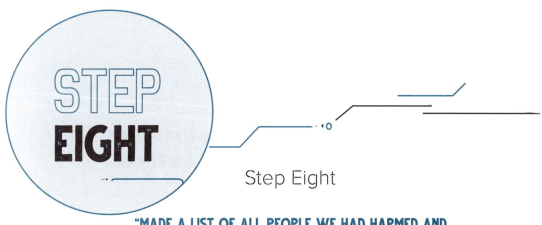

Step Eight

"MADE A LIST OF ALL PEOPLE WE HAD HARMED AND BECAME WILLING TO MAKE AMENDS TO THEM ALL."

MADE A LIST

Thus far, throughout the Twelve Steps, each step allows you to grow into your worthiness. We have made a decision to turn our lives over to the care of God and made a searching and fearless inventory. Now we come to a time when we are going to make a list.

OF ALL PEOPLE

Again, we are confronted with the word "all." "All" means 100 percent in this case. This includes people in your past and present that you may have victimized or hurt through your own worthlessness issues.

WE

Again it is very comforting to see the word "we" confirming that you are not the only person who may have caused others harm because of your worthless beliefs or behaviors. "Harm" is a difficult word for many people who struggle with worthless beliefs or behaviors. Harm is not something you ever want to cause, but believing in worthlessness does cause harm. It is here in Step Eight that we will address this. If you had done this Step earlier, in this workbook you probably would not have been aware enough to realize that your attitudes and behaviors actually inflicted pain whether knowingly or unknowingly. You may have caused some shame or hurt to many you have known, loved, and deeply cared about. It is now time to look at the harm that has been done to others while believing in worthlessness.

Let's take a moment and consider prayer, asking God to help you make this list. Make this list chronological. It is similar to your list in Step Four. Now would be a good time to go back to Step 4 and review the things you have done and the people you have hurt. Make a list of these people.

Ages 1-12

1. _____
2. _____
3. _____
4. _____
5. _____
6. _____
7. _____
8. _____

Ages 13-20

1. _____
2. _____
3. _____
4. _____
5. _____
6. _____
7. _____
8. _____
9. _____
10. _____

Ages 21-30

1. _____
2. _____
3. _____
4. _____
5. _____
6. _____
7. _____
8. _____
9. _____
10. _____

Ages 31-40

1. _____
2. _____
3. _____
4. _____
5. _____
6. _____
7. _____
8. _____
9. _____
10. _____

Ages 41-50

1. _____
2. _____
3. _____
4. _____
5. _____
6. _____
7. _____
8. _____
9. _____
10. _____

Ages 51-60

1. _____
2. _____
3. _____
4. _____
5. _____
6. _____
7. _____
8. _____
9. _____
10. _____

Ages 61 or older

1. _____
2. _____
3. _____
4. _____
5. _____
6. _____
7. _____
8. _____
9. _____
10. _____

Take time to compile a list of people you may have caused pain to more than once.

1. _____
2. _____
3. _____
4. _____
5. _____
6. _____
7. _____
11. _____
12. _____
13. _____
14. _____
15. _____
16. _____
17. _____

8._____ 18._____

9._____ 19._____

10._____ 20._____

AND

"And" is a great conjunction. I am glad that we didn't stop at just making this list. If we did, it would be possibly too painful to bear.

How do you feel about making your list?

I feel _____ .   I feel _____ .

BECAME

This is a process. It takes time. Give yourself permission to become willing to make amends. This is similar to Step Four and Five where you are reckoning a part of yourself. How did you feel after you completed Step Five?

I felt _____ .   I felt _____ .

WILLING

We have talked about the word "willing" indirectly in Step Six when we discussed being "entirely ready." "Willing" means that you are, regardless of emotion, willing to submit or comply with what needs to be done. This doesn't mean that you are going to do it yet, just that you are willing. For those who exercise, it is similar to lying in bed and at some point becoming willing to get up and move in the direction of exercising. We don't arrive at the gym immediately, but we do begin moving in that direction.

What are some experiences you have had in becoming willing during your learning process so far?

_____

_____

_____

What were the results of this willingness?

_____

_____

_____

MAKE AMENDS

Making an amend is making something right again, to restore or try to mend something that has been broken. Many of us will do this as we move from our Step Eight to our Step Nine. Part of Step Eight is that we become willing to make that step and mend what has been broken and acknowledge our responsibility in causing it to be broken.

TO THEM ALL

What percentage is "all"? _____%

Make a list of these people again and write next to the name what percentage you are willing to make an amend.

1._____	_____%	11._____	_____%
2._____	_____%	12._____	_____%
3._____	_____%	13._____	_____%
4._____	_____%	14._____	_____%
5._____	_____%	15._____	_____%
6._____	_____%	16._____	_____%
7._____	_____%	17._____	_____%
8._____	_____%	18._____	_____%
9._____	_____%	19._____	_____%
10._____	_____%	20._____	_____%

Use this list regularly until you become 100 percent willing to make amends to them all. Prayerfully consider this as you become willing.

Some people stay at Step Eight for some time until they become willing to make amends to them all. There are some experiences that are quite painful. Step Eight is meant to get us to the point where we are willing. In the space that follows, write the date when you became 100 percent willing to make amends to every person on this list. _____

What is the most significant thing you have learned about yourself in completing your Step Eight?

_____

_____

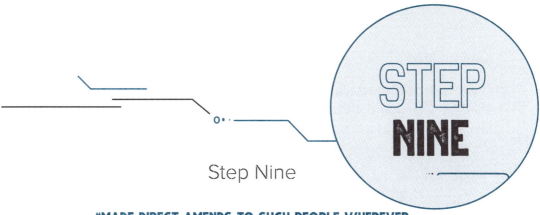

Step Nine

"MADE DIRECT AMENDS TO SUCH PEOPLE WHEREVER POSSIBLE, EXCEPT WHEN TO DO SO WOULD INJURE THEM OR OTHERS."

MADE

This is the last time the word "made" is used in our Twelve Step journey, and it may also be the most painful. Now we will turn our energies, creativity, and time into making direct amends to those we have harmed because of our worthless beliefs or behaviors.

DIRECT

What are some words you think of when you hear the word "direct"?

1._____ 3._____

2._____ 4._____

What are some words that come to mind that are opposite of "direct"?

1._____ 3._____

2._____ 4._____

"Direct" is definitely the straightest line between any two points. In the past many people who struggle with worthless beliefs or behaviors have been vague, shamed, and blamed, and have avoided and rationalized many behaviors. Some defense mechanisms may have been for the purpose of blaming others for their behaviors. Some rationalized why they behaved that way and why they weren't responsible. Some minimized their behaviors and were not able to see the damage done in other people's lives. These defense mechanisms helped them quite a bit to stay in worthless beliefs or behaviors, but they hold no hope on the path to worthy. Let's discuss what "direct" means.

The most direct formula as it relates to these amends is as follows:

1. **Face-to-face contact:** Talk to the person, face-to-face, and have a discussion regarding what you did that caused them harm. This is the most direct amend that can be made in a relationship. This is by far the best method of being direct with your amends.

2. **Phone Calls:** If the person is too far away for you to travel to them and make a direct amend, then a phone call can suffice as a second-most-direct amend.

3. **Letter:** For the person who does not have a phone, or cannot be reached in any other manner, a letter is your least direct amend. However, consider that anything written or sent by e-mail or text can be passed along. I would get advice before sending a letter or e-mail.

4. **Symbolic:** Symbolically put the person you are making an amend to in an empty chair facing you and make your amend to them. This would be only for people you don't know or can't contact. Do not use a symbolic amend for nonsexual offenses unless you consult your sponsor or therapist. However, a symbolic amend is totally appropriate for sexual relationships prior to marriage or outside of the marriage.

AMENDS

Making amends is a process of fusing two pieces that are broken and bringing them into contact. You are not required to restore the relationship. An amend is you cleaning your side of the street. It does not minimize, rationalize, or blame anyone for the behavior that caused pain. It is you looking fully at the pain that you caused another human being and acknowledging that pain to them. It is asking them to forgive you and advance in the relationship as they wish to. You are not responsible for their forgiveness. You are only 100 percent responsible for what you did to them.

A word of caution: You may need the help of the group or a therapist to help you decide whom you should or should not see. Going to see ex-lovers you were involved with prior to your present marriage is not a good idea.

SUCH PEOPLE

Make a list of the people from Step Eight and in the columns provided check off those you can amend face-to-face, with a call, by sending a letter, or with a symbolic amend.

NAME	FACE-TO-FACE	CALL	LETTER	SYMBOLIC
1.				
2.				
3.				
4.				
5.				
6.				
7.				
8.				
9.				
10.				
11.				
12.				
13.				
14.				
15.				
16.				
17.				
18.				
19.				
20.				

WHEREVER POSSIBLE

In the 1930s, when the Steps were written, "wherever possible" was much more limited than today. Today "wherever possible" is almost everywhere due to planes and technology that enable us to reach anyone in the world. The wording "wherever possible" also acknowledges the fact that not everyone to whom you owe an amend can be reached, found, or located. For this you are not responsible. If you can't locate someone, you are no longer responsible to make that amend. If you feel you need to make a symbolic amend, you can write them a letter and read it to them as if they were in a chair in front of you. This may be helpful for you to resolve the issue.

List those people whom, after trying, you were not able to locate.

1._____   5._____
2._____   6._____
3._____   7._____
4._____   8._____

EXCEPT

"Except" appears to be one of the bigger words to some people who struggle with worthless beliefs or behaviors during this Step. Many worthless beliefs or behaviors say, "Oh, good, a loophole." However, this is not what the word "except" means. This word is used very sparingly. It means that there are some on the list that need to be exceptions. List those who you currently believe would be exceptions because to make them aware of these issues now would cause them injury or harm.

1._____   4._____
2._____   5._____
3._____   6._____

List four people you respect who have already done their Step Nine.

1._____   3._____
2._____   4._____

After talking to each person you listed above, what are their perceptions of whether your list of exceptions is appropriate? After considering their feedback, list those who still need to be considered exempt.

_____
_____
_____

What is the injury or harm that would be caused if you made an amend to those on your above list?

_____
_____
_____

After prayer and meditation, do you have peace about those people not receiving a direct amend?

Yes _____   No _____

Make a list again of the people you owe amends to. In the column next to their name, list the date you made your amend. *Caution:* Do not wait—actively pursue this!

NAME   **DATE**

1. _____   _____
2. _____   _____
3. _____   _____
4. _____   _____
5. _____   _____
6. _____   _____
7. _____   _____
8. _____   _____
9. _____   _____
10. _____   _____
11. _____   _____
12. _____   _____

13. _____   _____
14. _____   _____
15. _____   _____
16. _____   _____
17. _____   _____
18. _____   _____
19. _____   _____
20. _____   _____

Complete your Step Nine by filling in the dates related to all the people on this list. Your Step Nine is not complete until the last date is listed.

How many direct amends can you make in the next week? Month? Three months?

1 Week _____   1 Month _____   3 Months _____

What were some of the experiences you had in doing your Step Nine?

_____

_____

_____

What were some of the feelings you had before, during, and after making your amends?

Before, I felt _____.

During, I felt _____.

After, I felt _____.

How do you feel about these relationships now, after you have made your amends?

I feel _____.   I feel _____.

What is the most significant thing you learned about yourself while completing your Step Nine?

_____

_____

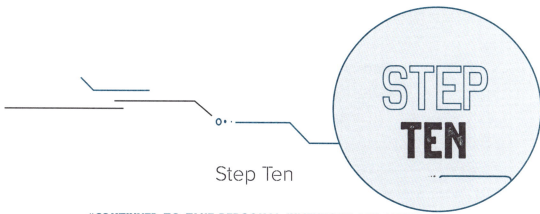

Step Ten

"CONTINUED TO TAKE PERSONAL INVENTORY AND WHEN WE WERE WRONG, PROMPTLY ADMITTED IT."

CONTINUED

"Continue" is a process that will last a lifetime. Being human means making mistakes. Step Ten allows us to be human without accumulating guilt or shame from behavior or attitudes. Step Ten is a lifestyle. What is the date you are starting this lifestyle choice?

Date _____

PERSONAL INVENTORY

A personal inventory is a recording of a person's behavior and attitudes. Behavior and attitudes can hurt us, as well as others. The other side of our inventory is strengths we may have practiced today. Our becoming worthy will enable strengths to grow. In Step Ten, we don't have to proclaim our strengths to others. This is for us to know and to thank God for. In Step Ten we are honest about our mistakes and then admit them to those who were affected by our mistakes.

Below is a form to use over the next month so that you can get into a healthy habit and make sure that this principle is being applied regularly in your life. You are going to need to continue this behavior throughout your life. Now that we are shameless, we can relate to God more openly than ever before in our recovery.

Your personal inventory is not up at the end of the month. This form is available only to help you get into the habit of looking honestly at yourself without shame, and to help you to say, "That was a mistake," and admit it promptly.

Day	Amends Asked For	Strength Acknowledged
1		
2		
3		
4		
5		
6		
7		
8		
9		
10		
11		
12		
13		
14		
15		
16		
17		
18		
19		
20		
21		
22		
23		
24		
25		
26		
27		
28		
29		
30		
31		

"Promptly" means in a timely manner. It does not mean weeks or months later. It should not be much longer than the day you made the mistake. Admit it to yourself and the other person and move on. How long did it take you to make your amends after you were aware that you needed to? (Write in the time it took in the blank space next to "Day ____.")

What is the average time it took you to make an amend? _____

Does the above time fit your definition for prompt? Yes _____   No _____

If your answer is no, what is your plan to improve your promptness? Ask five people you know who have done their Step Ten how they worked on promptness. Record your findings below.

_____
_____
_____

What is the most significant thing you learned about yourself in completing your Step Ten?

_____
_____

Step Eleven

"SOUGHT THROUGH PRAYER AND MEDITATION TO IMPROVE OUR CONSCIOUS CONTACT WITH GOD AS WE UNDERSTOOD HIM, PRAYING ONLY FOR THE KNOWLEDGE OF HIS WILL FOR US AND THE POWER TO CARRY THAT OUT."

As we walk on the road to worthy, many behaviors and beliefs have changed along the way. As you enter Step Eleven, you'll see we are being asked to focus on two different behaviors, prayer and meditation. On the next page is a chart for keeping track of your participation in these two behaviors as you work on your Step Eleven.

SOUGHT

Sought means to seek with the intention to find. This takes time and effort. Do you put time aside to pray and meditate on a regular basis?

Yes _____ No _____

If your answer is no, set aside time to do this daily. Once this time is set, you may or may not want to involve another person to make sure that you are accountable. If you choose to do this, what is their name?

_____

Below, check if you were able to pray and/or meditate on a daily basis for the thirty-one days.

Day	Prayer	Meditation
1		
2		
3		
4		
5		
6		
7		
8		
9		
10		
11		
12		
13		
14		
15		
16		
17		
18		
19		
20		
21		
22		
23		
24		
25		
26		
27		
28		
29		
30		
31		

CONSCIOUS CONTACT

What have been some of your "contact" experiences over the last thirty-one days?

_____
_____
_____

Some people journal their contacts with God. Would you like to make that a part of your spiritual life?

Yes _____   No _____

KNOWLEDGE OF HIS WILL

Other questions to ask yourself are, "Am I praying for the knowledge of His will?" If you feel you are doing this, put a Y next to the days you are praying. As a Christian, this probably is already a part of your life. In this step, it is a specific focus on our road to worthy.

What knowledge of His will have you gained over the last thirty-one days?

_____
_____
_____

In what ways has God given you the power to carry out His will, as you have understood it, during the last thirty-one days? Be specific.

_____
_____
_____

What is the most significant thing you learned about yourself in completing your Step Eleven?

_____
_____

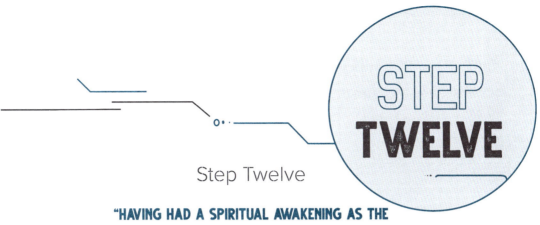

Step Twelve

"HAVING HAD A SPIRITUAL AWAKENING AS THE RESULT OF THESE STEPS, WE TRIED TO CARRY THIS MESSAGE TO OTHERS, AND TO PRACTICE THESE PRINCIPLES IN ALL OUR AFFAIRS."

HAVING HAD A SPIRITUAL AWAKENING

In many ways recovery from worthless beliefs or behaviors has brought on several awakenings, all of which are spiritual. What are some awakenings you have had in your spiritual life since you started your road to worthy?

_____
_____
_____
_____
_____
_____

What part of these awakenings was a direct result of working the Steps?

_____
_____

Which Steps seemed to be more important to you related to a spiritual awakening?

_____
_____

TRIED TO CARRY THIS MESSAGE TO OTHERS

How have you tried to carry this message to others during your walk on the road to worthy?

_____
_____
_____

What are some things you have learned about yourself and others as you have carried the message to others?

_____
_____
_____
_____

What are some experiences you have had in "giving it away"?

_____
_____
_____
_____

How did you feel after giving it away?

I felt _____.   I felt _____.

AND TO PRACTICE THESE PRINCIPLES IN ALL OUR AFFAIRS

Continuing the principles of honesty, spirituality, and responsibility for your own behavior, good or bad, and being prompt about admitting it, is important for a lifestyle of recovery. This helps you avoid carrying around guilt and shame that can bring you back into a cycle of worthless beliefs or behaviors. You deserve the best worthy feelings that you could ever have. It is in "giving it away" that you will often find that your own healing is enhanced.

How have you practiced these principles in the following areas of your life?

Spiritual Life

1. _____   3. _____
2. _____   4. _____

Emotional Life

1. _____ 3. _____
2. _____ 4. _____

Social Life

1. _____ 3. _____
2. _____ 4. _____

Physical Health/Exercise

1. _____ 3. _____
2. _____ 4. _____

Financially

1. _____ 3. _____
2. _____ 4. _____

Parenting

1. _____ 3. _____
2. _____ 4. _____

Work Relationships

1. _____ 3. _____
2. _____ 4. _____

Family Members

1. _____ 3. _____
2. _____ 4. _____

Sexuality

1. _____ 3. _____
2. _____ 4. _____

Marriage

1. _____ 3. _____
2. _____ 4. _____

What is the most significant thing you learned about yourself while completing Step Twelve?

_____
_____

The Twelve Steps of Alcoholics Anonymous

1. We admitted we were powerless over alcohol—that our lives had become unmanageable.

2. Came to believe that a Power greater than ourselves could restore us to sanity.

3. Made a decision to turn our will and our lives over to the care of God as we understood Him.

4. Made a searching and fearless moral inventory of ourselves.

5. Admitted to God, to ourselves, and to another human being the exact nature of our wrongs.

6. Were entirely ready to have God remove all these defects of character.

7. Humbly asked Him to remove our shortcomings.

8. Made a list of all people we had harmed, and became willing to make amends to them all.

9. Made direct amends to such people wherever possible, except when to do so would injure them or others.

10. Continued to take personal inventory, and when we were wrong, promptly admitted it.

11. Sought though prayer and meditation to improve our conscious contact with God as we understood Him, praying only for knowledge of His will for us and the power to carry that out.

12. Having had a spiritual awakening as the result of these steps, we tried to carry this message to others and to practice these principles in all our affairs.

The Twelve-Steps reprinted for adaptation by permission of AA World Services, Inc. Copyright 1939.

The Twelve Steps of Alcoholics Anonymous
adapted for people who struggle with worthless beliefs or behaviors

1. We admitted we were powerless over our worthless beliefs or behaviors—that our lives had become unmanageable.
2. Came to believe that a Power greater than ourselves could restore us to sanity.
3. Made a decision to turn our will and our lives over to the care of God as we understood Him.
4. Made a searching and fearless moral inventory of ourselves.
5. Admitted to God, to ourselves, and to another human being the exact nature of our wrongs.
6. Were entirely ready to have God remove all these defects of character.
7. Humbly asked God to remove our shortcomings.
8. Made a list of all people we had harmed, and became willing to make amends to them all.
9. Made direct amends to such people wherever possible, except when to do so would injure them or others.
10. Continued to take personal inventory, and when we were wrong, promptly admitted it.
11. Sought through prayer and meditation to improve our conscious contact with God as we understood Him, praying only for knowledge of His will for us and the power to carry that out.
12. Having had a spiritual awakening as the result of these steps, we tried to carry this message to others and to practice these principles in all our day-to-day living.

Feelings List

1. I feel (put word here) when (put a present situation when you feel this).
2. I first remember feeling (put the same feeling word here) when (explain earliest occurrence of this feeling)

RULES FOR COUPLES: 1- No examples about each other or the relationship. 2-Eye contact. 3-No feedback

Abandoned	Battered	Considerate	Distrusted	Goofy
Abused	Beaten	Consumed	Disturbed	Grateful
Aching	Beautiful	Content	Dominated	Greedy
Accepted	Belligerent	Cool	Domineering	Grief
Accused	Belittled	Courageous	Doomed	Grim
Accepting	Bereaved	Courteous	Doubtful	Grimy
Admired	Betrayed	Coy	Dreadful	Grouchy
Adored	Bewildered	Crabby	Eager	Grumpy
Adventurous	Blamed	Cranky	Ecstatic	Hard
Affectionate	Blaming	Crazy	Edgy	Harried
Agony	Bonded	Creative	Edified	Hassled
Alienated	Bored	Critical	Elated	Healthy
Aloof	Bothered	Criticized	Embarrassed	Helpful
Aggravated	Brave	Cross	Empowered	Helpless
Agreeable	Breathless	Crushed	Empty	Hesitant
Aggressive	Bristling	Cuddly	Enraged	High
Alive	Broken-up	Curious	Enraptured	Hollow
Alone	Bruised	Cut	Enthusiastic	Honest
Alluring	Bubbly	Damned	Enticed	Hopeful
Amazed	Burdened	Dangerous	Esteemed	Hopeless
Amused	Burned	Daring	Exasperated	Horrified
Angry	Callous	Dead	Excited	Hostile
Anguished	Calm	Deceived	Exhilarated	Humiliated
Annoyed	Capable	Deceptive	Exposed	Hurried
Anxious	Captivated	Defensive	Fake	Hurt
Apart	Carefree	Delicate	Fascinated	Hyper
Apathetic	Careful	Delighted	Feisty	Ignorant
Apologetic	Careless	Demeaned	Ferocious	Ignored
Appreciated	Caring	Demoralized	Foolish	Immature
Appreciative	Cautious	Dependent	Forced	Impatient
Apprehensive	Certain	Depressed	Forceful	Important
Appropriate	Chased	Deprived	Forgiven	Impotent
Approved	Cheated	Deserted	Forgotten	Impressed
Argumentative	Cheerful	Desirable	Free	Incompetent
Aroused	Childlike	Desired	Friendly	Incomplete
Astonished	Choked-up	Despair	Frightened	Independent
Assertive	Close	Despondent	Frustrated	Insecure
Attached	Cold	Destroyed	Full	Innocent
Attacked	Comfortable	Different	Funny	Insignificant
Attentive	Comforted	Dirty	Furious	Insincere
Attractive	Competent	Disenchanted	Gay	Isolated
Aware	Competitive	Disgusted	Generous	Inspired
Awestruck	Complacent	Disinterested	Gentle	Insulted
Badgered	Complete	Dispirited	Genuine	Interested
Baited	Confident	Distressed	Giddy	Intimate
Bashful	Confused	Distrustful	Giving	Intolerant

Copyright Douglas Weiss, Ph.D.   www.drdougweiss.com   719.278.3708

Involved	Panicked	Respected	Stiff	Under control
Irate	Paralyzed	Restless	Stimulated	Understanding
Irrational	Paranoid	Revolved	Stifled	Understood
Irked	Patient	Riled	Strangled	Undesirable
Irresponsible	peaceful	Rotten	Strong	Unfriendly
Irritable	Pensive	Ruined	Stubborn	Ungrateful
Irritated	Perceptive	Sad	Stuck	Unified
Isolated	Perturbed	Safe	Stunned	Unhappy
Jealous	Phony	Satiated	Stupid	Unimpressed
Jittery	Pleasant	Satisfied	Subdued	Unsafe
Joyous	Pleased	Scared	Submissive	Unstable
Lively	Positive	Scolded	Successful	Upset
Lonely	Powerless	Scorned	Suffocated	Uptight
Loose	Present	Scrutinized	Sure	Used
Lost	Precious	Secure	Sweet	Useful
Loving	Pressured	Seduced	Sympathy	Useless
Low	Pretty	Seductive	Tainted	Unworthy
Lucky	Proud	Self-centered	Tearful	Validated
Lustful	Pulled apart	Self-conscious	Tender	Valuable
Mad	Put down	Selfish	Tense	Valued
Maudlin	Puzzled	Separated	Terrific	Victorious
Malicious	Quarrelsome	Sensuous	Terrified	Violated
Mean	Queer	Sexy	Thrilled	Violent
Miserable	Quiet	Shattered	Ticked	Voluptuous
Misunder-	Raped	Shocked	Tickled	Vulnerable
stood	Ravished	Shot down	Tight	Warm
Moody	Ravishing	Shy	Timid	Wary
Morose	Real	Sickened	Tired	Weak
Mournful	Refreshed	Silly	Tolerant	Whipped
Mystified	Regretful	Sincere	Tormented	Whole
Nasty	Rejected	Sinking	Torn	Wicked
Nervous	Rejuvenated	Smart	Tortured	Wild
Nice	Rejecting	Smothered	Touched	Willing
Numb	Relaxed	Smug	Trapped	Wiped out
Nurtured	Relieved	Sneaky	Tremendous	Wishful
Nuts	Remarkable	Snowed	Tricked	Withdrawn
Obsessed	Remem-	Soft	Trusted	Wonderful
Offended	bered	Solid	Trustful	Worried
Open	Removed	Solitary	Trusting	Worthy
Ornery	Repulsed	Sorry	Ugly	Wounded
Out of control	Repulsive	Spacey	Unacceptable	Young
Overcome	Resentful	Special	Unapproach-	Zapped
Overjoyed	Resistant	Spiteful	able	
Overpowered	Responsible	Spontaneous	Unaware	
Overwhelmed	Responsive	Squelched	Uncertain	
Pampered	Repressed	Starved	Uncomfortable	

Affirmations

- ☐ I am a lovable person.
- ☐ I am able to experience my feelings today.
- ☐ I give myself permission to share my feelings with others today.
- ☐ I give myself permission to share myself with others.
- ☐ I have value.
- ☐ My partner also has value.
- ☐ I am a sexual person.
- ☐ My partner is a sexual person.
- ☐ I give myself permission to feel sexual toward my partner today.
- ☐ I give myself permission to ask for sexual intimacy today.
- ☐ I can trust myself.
- ☐ I can trust my partner.
- ☐ I am an intelligent person.
- ☐ My partner is an intelligent person.
- ☐ If I feel anger, I can talk about it directly.
- ☐ If I feel emotional pain, I give myself permission to talk to a safe person about it.
- ☐ Today, I can be free from withholding love, sex or money from those I love.
- ☐ I can celebrate others today with love, sex or money and time.
- ☐ I am sexual.
- ☐ As a part of who I am, I embrace my sexuality.
- ☐ I can learn to know others today.
- ☐ Today I can let others know me.

COUNSELING

"Without the intensive, my marriage would have ended and I would not have known why. Now I am happier than ever and my marriage is bonded permanently."

COUNSELING SESSIONS

Couples are helped through critical phases of disclosure moving into the process of recovery, and rebuilding trust in relationships. We have helped many couples rebuild their relationship and grasp and implement the necessary skills for an intimate relationship.

Individual counseling offers a personal treatment plan for successful healing in your life. In just one session a counselor can help you understand how you became stuck and how to move toward freedom.

Partners of sex addicts need an advocate. Feelings of fear, hurt, anger, betrayal, and grief require a compassionate, effective response. We provide that expert guidance and direction. We have helped many partners heal through sessions that get them answers to their many questions including: "How can I trust him again?"

A counseling session today can begin your personal journey toward healing.

3 AND 5 DAY INTENSIVES

in Colorado Springs, Colorado are available for the following issues:

- Sexual Addiction Couple or Individual
- Partners of Sexual Addicts
- Victims of Sexual Abuse
- Teenage Children of Sex Addicts
- Marriage Intensives
- Intimacy Anorexia
- Adult Children of Sex Addicts

ATTENDEES OF INTENSIVES WILL RECEIVE:
- Personal attention from counselors who specialize in your area of need
- An understanding of how the addiction /anorexia and its consequences came into being
- Three appointments daily
- Daily assignments to increase the productiveness of these daily sessions
- Individuals get effective counseling to recover from the effects of sexual addiction, abuse and anorexia
- Addiction, abuse, anorexia issues are thoroughly addressed for couples and individuals. This includes the effects on the partner or family members of the addict, and how to rebuild intimacy toward a stronger relationship.

NEW PRODUCTS

MOVING FORWARD

In this video, Dr. Doug Weiss uses his decades of experience helping women move forward after being divorced from their sexually addicted or intimacy anorexic husband to help you process your situation more effectively and intelligently.

DVD: $29.95

INDESTRUCTIBLE

The Indestructible video gives you a foundational understanding about your innate design as God's child. Addiction, betrayal, and abuse or neglected can all cause trials in our lives that can trigger feelings of worthlessness and defeat.

DVD: $29.00

SEX AFTER RECOVERY

Sex after Recovery will help you navigate a variety of issues including how to reclaim a healthy sexual life together. This DVD set will help you to reclaim and recover your sexuality both individually and with each other.

DVD: $59.95

NEW PRODUCTS

HEALING HER HEART AFTER RELAPSE

Relapse doesn't have to occur, but if it happens, knowing how to navigate it intelligently can make a huge difference in a marriage. Each relapse impacts the wife significantly. Every couple in recovery would do well to have these tools before a potential relapse.

DVD: $29.95

PAIN FOR LOVE

Pain For Love describes in detail one of the most insidious strategies of an intimacy anorexic with their spouse. This dynamic is experienced by many who are married to an intimacy anorexic. This paradigm can empower the spouse and help them stop participating in a pain for love dynamic in their marriage.

DVD: $29.95

SIN OF WITHHOLDING

This DVD is the first to address the Biblical foundation of the sin of withholding in believers' hearts. The practical application in marriage addressing Intimacy Anorexia is also interwoven in this revelational teaching on the Sin of Withholding. Once a believer is free of this sin, their walk with the Lord and their fruit towards others can increase expediently.

DVD: $49.95

MEN'S RECOVERY

This book gives more current information than many professional counselors have today. In addition to informing sex addicts and their partners about sex addiction, it gives hope for recovery. The information provided in this book would cost hundreds of dollars in counseling hours to receive. Many have attested to successful recovery from this information alone.

BOOK: $22.95
CD: $35.00

101 FREEDOM EXERCISES

This is the best single resource for the Christian who desires to know what they need to do to get and stay free from sexual addiction. This book contains 101 exercises that have been proven to work.

WORKBOOK: $39.95

STEPS TO FREEDOM

This is a Christian approach to the Twelve Steps. This book will guide you through the 12 Steps of recovery that have been helpful for many addicted people. This book is specifically written for the person desiring recovery from sexual addiction.

STEP BOOK: $14.95

HELPING HER HEAL

The *Helping Her Heal* DVD is for the man who has disclosed his sexual addiction to his partner or spouse. This DVD offers practical tools for hearing her pain, navigating her grief and losses, discovering her expectations of you and the boundaries she may need to heal.

DVD: $69.95
DVD COMPANION GUIDE: $11.95

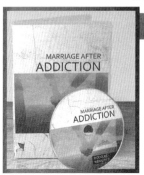

MARRIED AFTER ADDICTION

Addiction can have devastating effects on even good marriages. In this DVD you are intelligently guided through the journey you will experience if addiction is part of your marriage story. You will learn important information about the early and later stages of recovery for your marriage.

DVD: $29.95

WOMEN'S RECOVERY

Partners: Healing From His Addiction book is the latest in research of the affects on a woman who has lived with a sexual addict. The riveting statistics combined with personal stories of recovery make this a must read book for any woman in a relationship with a sex addict. This book gives you hope and a beginning plan for personal recovery.

BOOK: $14.95

PARTNER'S RECOVERY GUIDE

This is like therapy in a box for women who want to walk through the residual effects of being in a relationship with a sex addict.

WORKBOOK: $39.95

BEYOND LOVE

This is an interactive workbook that allows the partners of sex addicts to gain insight and strength through working the Twelve Steps.

STEP BOOK: $14.95

HE NEEDS TO CHANGE, DR. WEISS

He Needs To Change, Dr. Weiss DVD addresses the pain, trauma, and betrayal women experience because of their partner's sex addiction, betrayal, and/or intimacy anorexia. In this DVD, Dr. Weiss addresses the issue of change that he has explained to thousands of women in his office.

DVD: $29.95

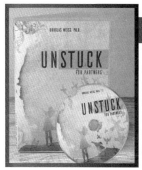

UNSTUCK FOR PARTNERS

The *Unstuck* DVD is for every woman who has experienced the pain of their partner's sex addiction or intimacy anorexia and feels stuck, confused, frustrated and unable to move on. You didn't sign up for this and honestly, you don't get it! This DVD helps you "get it" so you can process the painful reality you are in and start to live again.

DVD: $29.95

TRIGGERED

Triggers are normal for partners of sex addicts, but each woman's triggers are unique and must be navigated in different ways. This DVD can be a life-changing message which will validate your struggles to heal and help you face the challenges of being triggered after partner betrayal trauma.

DVD: $49.00

DISCLOSURE

Disclosure is one of the most important topics in sexual addiction recovery. In this DVD, Dr. Weiss discusses the various types of disclosure. Each type of disclosure is for a specific purpose or person. This DVD can expedite the understanding of each of the significant processes of disclosure for the addict, the spouse and the marriage.

DVD: $39.95

PARTNER BETRAYAL TRAUMA

Partner Betrayal Trauma is real. Your pain and experience of betrayal has impacted all of your being and all of your relationships.

The book, DVD set, Workbook and Step guide were designed to help guide you thoughtfully through your own personal healing from the effects of being betrayed by your spouse or significant other. The pain and trauma of being betrayed, especially sexual betrayal, by a spouse or significant other is multidimensional and multifaceted. Your pain and trauma are real and these resources will help you in your journey of recovery from Partner Betrayal Trauma.

BOOK: $22.95   DVD: $65.95   WORKBOOK: $39.95   STEPBOOK: $14.95

INTIMACY ANOREXIA

This hidden addiction is destroying so many marriages today. In your hands is the first antidote for someone with intimacy anorexia to turn the pages on this addiction process. Excerpts from intimacy anorexics and their spouses help this book become clinically helpful and personal in its impact to communicate hope and healing for the intimacy anorexic and the marriage.

BOOK: $22.95
DVD: $69.95

INTIMACY ANOREXIA: THE WORKBOOK

This is like therapy in a box. Inside is 100 exercises that have already been proven helpful in treating intimacy anorexia.

WORKBOOK: $39.95

INTIMACY ANOREXIA: THE STEPS

This is the only twelve step workbook just for intimacy anorexia. Each step gives you progress in your healing from intimacy anorexia.
STEP BOOK: $14.95

MARRIED & ALONE

This is for the spouse of an intimacy anorexic. You feel disconnected, untouched and often unloved. You are not crazy and Dr. Weiss will help you to start a journey of recovery from living with a spouse with intimacy anorexia.

BOOK: $14.95
DVD: $49.95

MARRIED & ALONE: HEALING EXERCISES FOR SPOUSES

This is the first workbook to offer practical suggestions and techniques to better navigate through recovery from your spouse's Intimacy Anorexia.
WORKBOOK: $39.95

MARRIED & ALONE: THE TWELVE STEP GUIDE

This Twelve Step guide will help the spouse of an intimacy anorexic work through the Twelve Steps that many others have found to be helpful in their recovery.

STEP BOOK: $14.95

MARRIAGE RESOURCES

LOVER SPOUSE

Lover Spouse helps you understand marriage from a Christ-centered perspective. Christian Marriages were designed to be different, passionate, fulfilling, and long-lasting.   BOOK: $13.95

UPGRADE YOUR SEX LIFE

Upgrade Your Sex Life actually teaches you own unique sexual expression that you and your partner are pre-wired to enjoy.
BOOK: $16.95

SERVANT MARRIAGE

Servant Marriage book is a Revelation on God's Masterpiece of marriage. In these pages, you will walk with God as He creates the man, the woman and his masterpiece called marriage.
BOOK: $13.95

MARRIAGE MONDAYS

This is an eight week marriage training that actually gives you the skills to have a healthy and more vibrant marriage.
BOOK: $16.95

INTIMACY

This 100 Day guide can transform couples from any level of intimacy to a lifestyle of satiation with their spouse.   BOOK: $11.95

MIRACLE OF MARRIAGE

God made your marriage to be an amazing and unique miracle. Dr. Weiss walks you through the creation and maintenance of your marriage. You will be exposed to a practical insights that can help make your marriage into God's original design.
DVD: $12.95

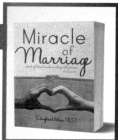

OTHER RESOURCES

WORTHY: EXERCISES & STEP BOOK

The *Worthy* Workbook and DVD, is designed for a 12 week study. Here is a path that anyone can take to get and stay worthy. Follow this path, and you too will make the journey from worthless to worthy just as others have.

DVD: $29.95
BOOK: $29.95

EMOTIONAL FITNESS

Everyone has an unlimited number of emotions, but few have been trained to identify, choose, communicate, and master them. More than a guide for gaining emotional fitness and mastery, in these pages you will find a pathway to a much more fulfilling life.

BOOK: $16.95

LETTERS TO MY DAUGHTER

A gift for your daugher as she enters college. *Letters to my Daughter* includes my daily letters to my daughter during her first year of college.

BOOK: $14.95

BORN FOR WAR

Born for War teaches practical tools to defeat these sexual landmines and offers scriptural truths that empower young men to desire successfulness in the war thrust upon them.

DVD: $29.95

PRINCES TAKE LONGER THAN FROGS

This 2 hour DVD helps single women ages 15-30, to successfully navigate through the season of dating.

DVD: $29.95

SUCCESSFULLY SINGLE

This 2 Disc DVD Series is definitely nothing you have heard before. Dr. Weiss charts new territory as to the why for sexual purity.

DVD: $29.95

SERIES FOR MEN

CLEAN

BOOK: $16.95
DVD: $29.95
JOURNAL: $16.95

Every Christian man is born into a sexual war. The enemy attacks the young, hoping to scar them permanently and leave them ruined. Your past is not enough to keep you from the enduringly clean life you want and deserve. This series can be used individually or in a small group setting.

LUST FREE LIVING

Every man can fight for and obtain a lust free lifestyle. Once you know how to stop lust, you will realize how weak lust really can be. God gace you the power to protect those you love from the ravages of lust for the rest of your life! It's time to take it back!

BOOK: $13.95
DVD: $23.95

MEN MAKE MEN

Dr. Weiss takes the listeners by the hand and step-by-step walks through the creative process God used to make every man into a man of God. This practical teaching on DVD combined with the Men Make Guidebook can revitalize the men in any home or local church.

DVD: $29.95
GUIDEBOOK: $11.95

A·A·S·A·T
American Association for Sex Addiction Therapy

SEX ADDICTION TRAINING SET

Both men and women are seeking to counsel more than ever for sexually addictive behaviors. You can be prepared! Forty-seven hours of topics related to sexual addiction treatment are covered in this training including:
- The Six Types of Sex Addicts
- Neurological Understanding
- Sex and Recovery
- Relapse Strategies

TRAINING SET: $1195

PARTNER'S RECOVERY TRAINING SET

With this AASAT training, you will gain proven clinical insight into treating the issues facing partners. You can be prepared! Thirty-nine hours of topics related to partners treatment are covered in this training, including:
- Partner Model
- Partner Grief
- Anger
- Boundaries

TRAINING SET: $995

INTIMACY ANOREXIA TRAINING SET

This growing issue of Intimacy Anorexia will need your competent help in your community. Now, you can be prepared to identify it and treat it. In this training you'll cover topics like:
- Identifying Intimacy Anorexia
- Causes of Intimacy Anorexia
- Treatment Plan
- Relapse Strategies

TRAINING SET: $995

FOR MORE INFORMATION VISIT WWW.AASAT.ORG OR CALL 719.330.2425

Heart to Heart Counseling Center has recently acquired Cereset, the most technologically advanced neuromodulation software available. It has received 13 peer review publications, and 9 Institutional Review Boards (IRB) clinically approved trials including the US Military.

By rebalancing and recalibrating the brain, it has helped anxiety, PTSD, trauma, sleeplessness, addiction, low mood and energy, TBI, stress management and neuroplasticity in many of my clients. Most spouses at Heart to Heart Counseling Center have many of the PTSD symptoms from betrayal. More than 80% of those with addiction have unresolved traumas as part of their story.

The brain is your central command center. When your brain is out of balance, or stuck, you don't feel right and it's impossible to function at your highest level. Cereset is a proven technology that's non-invasive and highly effective. Cereset can help your brain free itself, enabling you to achieve higher levels of well-being and balance throughout your life.

Here's what clients had to say about Cereset Garden of the Gods after their sessions:

> "I'm waking up earlier and feeling more rested and alert. Anxiety is lessened. PTSD symptoms alleviated. Lessened food cravings and quantity of food reduced. Arthritis symptoms improved. I feel more relaxed, less angry and reactive."

The cost for five sessions (one per day) is $1,500.

For more information call us at 719-278-3708